T0158899

RECIPE FOR
ORGANIZATIONAL SUCCESS

RECIPE FOR ORGANIZATIONAL SUCCESS

A Ten-Step Methodology to Build a
World-Class-Performing Organization

Bharat Desai

RECIPE FOR ORGANIZATIONAL SUCCESS
A TEN-STEP METHODOLOGY TO BUILD A WORLD-
CLASS-PERFORMING ORGANIZATION

iUniverse books may be ordered through booksellers or by contacting

iUniverse
1663 Liberty Drive
Bloomington, IN 47403
www.iuniverse.com
1-800-Authors (1-800-288-4677)

ISBN: 978-1-5320-0670-8 (sc)
ISBN: 978-1-5320-0669-2 (e)

Library of Congress Control Number: 2016914924

Print information available on the last page.

iUniverse rev. date: 12/06/2016

To my parents, who helped me become the person I am today

CONTENTS

ACKNOWLEDGMENTS

There are many acknowledgments due when a book represents more than thirty-five years of experience, research, thoughts, and discussions. Because this book reflects so many years of work, it is impossible to even name, much less express my appreciation to, all the individuals who have helped.

I would like to thank Dave Orton, Tony Alvarez, Dan Gilbert, and Ted Tewksbury for encouraging me to write this book and for believing in me. These successful high-tech top executives' pointed comments and feedback were greatly appreciated.

Thanks to all the leaders, peers, and staff I've had the pleasure to work with during my professional career. They have trained, coached, taught, guided, and encouraged me, and I have learned a lot from them.

Over the last five years, I've listened to many professional webinars. I'm grateful to all of those who have taken their time to share their knowledge, most of whom are book authors. I learned a lot from these and other authors, whose ideas are expressed throughout this book.

Thanks to my wife; our two daughters, Shalini and Shivani; and our sons-in-law, Mayur and Amish, who have encouraged me to write this book and have edited my initial work.

Finally, I would like to thank the organizations and leaders that have allowed me to interact with them, as well as each of you reading this book. I hope you enjoy it.

INTRODUCTION

The seeds of this book were planted about twenty years ago, as I started to document my experiences about running an organization effectively and efficiently—what worked and what needed improvement.

While growing up in India, I always knew I wanted to become an engineer because I excelled at math and was a very logical thinker. I fulfilled my desire by becoming an electrical engineer. After graduating, I started to work for a state-owned utility company. As soon as I began my career, I learned that I wanted to get things done faster and better while others were taking it easy. When I questioned others about their casual attitude toward work, I was told this was how things were done in government.

Hoping for a more fulfilling experience, I left that job to join a private company, a chemical plant, in my hometown, Ahmedabad, in the state of Gujarat. To my surprise, I found a similar environment there. A few years later, I grabbed an opportunity to immigrate to the United States in 1976. Since then, I have worked for eleven electronics companies, from start-ups to Fortune 500 companies, and risen through the ranks, starting as an engineer and becoming a vice president of operations.

While working for a variety of US companies, I realized that while organizations functioned much better in the United States than in India, they still needed improvement. I began making observations on how to run an organization most effectively and efficiently, focusing on what key processes and systems are needed to achieve this goal. I became passionate about building high-performing operations and became a continuous-improvement person—personally and professionally. For example, I sought to continuously advance my skills, so I received MSEE and MBA degrees while handling full family responsibilities and working full-time. In order to improve an organization's performance, I came up with a methodology, an elegant solution to meet operational challenges. The methodology is a blueprint to build world-class-performing organizations.

This book is a humble attempt to translate my more than thirty-five years of experience and the experiences of other successful business leaders into a foundation for useful action by fast-paced business executives.

While today's business leaders deal with complex business problems, they struggle to find time to apply sound management principles to achieve organizational excellence, which means the organization has improved profitability, has improved capability (preparation for sustained long-term performance), and has become a world-class-performing organization. Such an organization creates a culture of accountability, discipline, and systems, and it consequently accomplishes more by doing less.

Why It's Hard to Build a World-Class-Performing Organization

Most organizations talk about achieving lowest possible cost and improving execution but often fall short of these objectives. Why? First of all, they do not use effective systems and processes for major business functions. Next, they do not create a culture of continuous improvement. Finally, these organizations have not built a culture of discipline and accountability. These are the characteristics of world-class-performing organizations, and companies must work hard to build these characteristics into their organizations.

The root cause of the underperformance of any organization can be traced to one or more of the following hard business truths:

1. *Status quo:* The organization is content to keep things as is and does not like change. Status quo is a recipe for failure. If you stay with it, things will inevitably decline.
2. *Denial:* The organization does not want to accept the reality of the situation. Denial is the reaction of an organization in trouble.
3. *Absence of written plans:* Remember—if you fail to plan, you plan to fail. This is a recipe for disaster.

Do you know any organizations that suffer from the above characteristics? Would you describe them as overperforming organizations? Evidence of such organizations are listed below.

1. New product introductions get delayed.
2. Execution is not the core element of the organizational culture.
3. Low employee and organizational productivity are the norm.
4. Inferior products get introduced.
5. Cost structure, product cost, and gross profit margin are all inadequate.
6. Operations infrastructure is suboptimal.
7. Time-to-market opportunities are missed.
8. A corporate continuous improvement process is lacking or not well-defined.
9. Some systems and processes for major business functions are ineffective.

The ten-step methodology in this book, a collection of solid management principles and practices, is a proven business model that can easily be added to just about any operating business. It will produce successful outcomes, even under the most difficult of circumstances, because it is an old-school approach that focuses on fundamentals.

The methodology is based on the following three principles:

1. Keep it simple. In most cases, simple is better than complex.
2. Learn to focus and manage priorities. For example, focus only on the top three priorities at a time.
3. Top leadership must make unwavering relentless commitment to bring operational transformation.

This book will help improve the organizational performance of your organization. It concentrates on key business processes related to people, leadership, execution, cost structure, and problem solving, and it addresses challenges in these functions. The book provides practical solutions in the form of strategies, models, systems, processes, tools, and techniques.

By applying the principles in this book, you can improve profitability, improve preparation for a sustained, long-term performance, and build a world-class organization.

Other benefits are the following:

1. Continuous improvement will be your new corporate mantra.
2. You will achieve long-term superior financial and operating performance.
3. You will promote systems thinking and bring operational transformation that will lead to exponential growth for your employees and the organization.
4. You will shift the thinking of your organization and form good habits such as developing a culture of accountability and discipline.
5. You will create a path to achieve the best possible cost structure.
6. By using the corporate problem-solving tool, you will solve your most difficult organizational problems.
7. You will create a well-oiled organization that endures, allowing you to do well while doing good.
8. By exposing harsh realities, you will make meaningful progress in setting goals and objectives.
9. You will retain and develop talent.
10. You will develop operations expertise.

Overview of the Ten-Step Methodology

One of the biggest organizational challenges out there is to build a world-class-performing organization. I developed a specific methodology to meet this challenge. It is a collection of best business practices in the form of systems, models, processes, tools, and techniques that create an elegant solution to meet organizational challenges. It was developed with the characteristics of a world-class-performing organization in mind and what I have learned about best business practices from over thirty-five years of personal experience and that of my supervisors, my colleagues, my staff, industry leaders, and industry research.

In order to achieve sustainable change, you need to make two types of changes in your organization: people and leadership change and process change. The two types of changes are connected. Sustainable process change will never occur if people and leadership change does not occur. Sustainable change will only happen if the people and leadership change and process change occur simultaneously and with equal priority.

The first four steps of the methodology focus on people and leadership systems, and the remaining six steps focus on process changes related to execution, cost structure, and problem-solving business processes. I highly recommend that your organization concentrate 70 percent of its change efforts (priorities, time, money, and energy) on the first four steps of the methodology to make compelling progress. The first step of attaining unwavering, relentless commitment by the CEO is critical for the success of the methodology.

The methodology is based on creating a culture that makes deliberate continuous improvements by design, not by chance, through discipline and accountability. The methodology promotes systems thinking and brings operational transformation that leads to exponential growth for both the employees and the organization. Once implemented, it creates a high-performing, well-oiled organization that endures.

The methodology solves major problems associated with people, leadership, execution, cost structure, and problem-solving processes. It lays a solid foundation to improve short-term performance, and at the same time it builds, monitors, and sustains the long-term health of the organization.

Prerequisite: The methodology will only work if top leadership has made unwavering commitment to use the methodology and if the rules for building a world-class-performing organization are pursued. These rules are discussed in chapter 4 under step 3: Take Advantage of the Power of the Rule of Three.

Once implemented, the methodology works as follows: These steps create a culture of continuous improvement, which is all about thinking outside the box and finding ways to do things better. In a continuous improvement culture, employees' performance increases both immediately and over the long run as employees begin to use new techniques developed as a by-product of this new culture. This helps leaders design systems that enforce essential disciplines effectively. When the leaders ensure they are followed every day, at every level of the organization, the disciplines reinforce one another to create an adaptive organization that consistently generates the most value possible. The result is a high-performing, enduring organization.

Methodologies such as this have been available for some time to encourage a balanced approach, improve short-term performance, build the long-term health of the organization, and promote systems thinking. However, there are three main reasons that most organizations do not use such methodologies:

1. There is a lack of focus, commitment, and efforts to implement a methodology effectively.
2. The methodology is squeezed out by a focus on survival and by perceived pressure from investors.
3. There is an overemphasis on short-term results and an underemphasis on long-term value creation. Sometimes the board of directors may not fully comprehend company strategies. According to a report by McKinsey Research,[1] when asked which source of pressure was most responsible for their organizations' overemphasis on short-term financial results and underemphasis on long-term value creation, 47 percent of those surveyed cited the company's board.

While the thrust of the methodology implementation is relatively easy to articulate, *it's not easy to commit to and execute.* You'll be creating a deep shift in culture, behavior, and structure of your organization. Are you willing to do this to gain big returns?

---

[1] Nate Boaz and Erica Ariel Fox, "Change Leader, Change Thyself." *McKinsey Quarterly*, no. 4 (2014). Retrieved from McKinsey & Company.

Why Do You Want to Use the Methodology?

Once you implement the methodology, you will gain the following benefits:

- ❖ It helps you systematize and standardize everything. Standardization decreases ambiguity, increases predictability, and allows groups to function more effectively.
- ❖ It offers best business practices and models that produce the best performance outcome.
- ❖ It is all about doing the right things to get things done right. It shows you how to solve common problems. Solving problems is what effective management does.

In summary, the methodology helps you build a strong, ethical, and enduring organization.

In the coming pages, you will see a blueprint begin to develop for creating the foundation of a high-performing organization. The chapters provide practical solutions in the form of strategies, models, systems, processes, tools, and techniques. In short, the book shows you step-by-step how to build a world-class-performing organization and gives you the competitive advantage you need to succeed.

Food for Thought

1. Have you clearly identified your organization's top three operational challenges?
2. Do you have a methodology in place to build a world-class-performing organization?
3. On a scale of 1 to 10, how would you rate the execution of your organization?

CHAPTER 1

What Does a World-Class-Performing Organization Look Like?

World-class-performing organizations focus on five major business functions: people, leadership, execution, cost structure, and problem solving. They continuously, consistently, and proactively address challenges related to these functions to improve short-term performance and sustain the health of the organization, which is its capacity to deliver superior financial and operating performance over the long-term. It is also evidenced by how well an organization aligns, executes, and renews itself faster than all other organizations to stay ahead of the competition. In short, a world-class organization is a well-oiled organization that endures.

A well-oiled organization is one that makes running an organization effectively and efficiently a way of life, a strategic imperative. The organizational dynamics is a system of customer-supplier relationships. If this relationship is in alignment, that is, the need of a customer is met by the supplier, the effectiveness of the organization can be optimized. A well-oiled organization has all its organizational elements aligned. As Kilts, Lorber, and Manfredi say in their book *Doing What Matters,*[2] "The timing and movement of all components must be absolutely in sync. Even the slightest miss in timing will result in poor performance."

A well-oiled organization is one that endures and has a sense of purpose built around doing well by doing good, has a set of values or guiding

---

[2] James Kilts, Robert Lorber, and John Manfredi. *Doing What Matters: How to Get Results That Make a Difference* (New York City: Crown Business, 2007), 149.

principles known and used by all employees, has systemized everything, and is committed to nonstop growth.

Once created, such an organization runs on autopilot. It makes its competition sweat and toss at night. Such an organization will produce desired results efficiently and will create leaders at all levels, year in and year out. It will need fine-tuning from time to time. The reason organizations need fine-tuning is because there are internal and external factors that keep changing and the organization needs to adapt to these changes. This means they need to constantly adjust systems and processes to cope with the changing environment.

Attributes of a World-Class-Performing Organization

Numerous attributes are typical of all world-class-performing organizations:

- ❖ They are committed to continuous improvement.
- ❖ Their vision, strategy and goals are aligned.
- ❖ Striving is the cultural norm.
- ❖ All employees are accountable, disciplined, and satisfied.
- ❖ They accomplish more by doing less.
- ❖ They continuously and consistently improve.
- ❖ They operate at optimum/minimum cost.
- ❖ They align, execute, and renew themselves faster than the competition.
- ❖ They have improved capability.
- ❖ They use systems, models and/or methodologies.

Obstacles to Building World-Class-Performing Organizations

> *Obstacles are those frightful things you see when*
> *you take your eyes off your goals.*
> —unknown

There are several obstacles to building a world-class-performing organization. The major ones follow:

- ❖ lack of laser-sharp focus
- ❖ lack of operations expertise—most CEOs have either sales, marketing, finance, or technical backgrounds.
- ❖ unavailability of a step-by-step guide or some kind of methodology
- ❖ lack of unwavering commitment and dedicated efforts by top leadership
- ❖ too much focus on new product development
- ❖ too much focus on demand generation
- ❖ cost is an afterthought—treated as a tactical issue rather than a strategic one.
- ❖ the myth that there is not enough bandwidth (resources) to make process improvements

The first two elements are critical, so let's now discuss them in detail.

Lack of laser-sharp focus. Remember—execution starts with focus. Laser-sharp focus is achieved, first, by avoiding complexity and, second, by using the rule of three. Most organizations fail to understand the importance and power of the rule of three, so they do not use this rule effectively to get things done in their organizations. It is no accident that so far in our discussion we have used the rule of three. The methodology that we will be discussing is powerful yet simple because it is based on the rule of three. We will discuss the rule of three in detail in chapter 4.

Lack of operations expertise. Operations expertise means improving execution. There are two schools of thought about the best way to improve execution. One school emphasizes people, and the second school emphasizes process rather than people. Actually, the two schools are just two sides of the same coin. The methodology discussed here will show you how to take advantage of both schools.

To take care of the first (people) part, CEOs with sales/marketing/ technical/finance backgrounds should hire operations experts whenever possible. You may have heard that smart CEOs hire people smarter than themselves. In addition, the methodology outlined in this book will help develop operations expertise, including operations experts.

Secondly, organizations should use some kind of methodology like the one we are talking about to establish systems and processes.

Last but not least, as and when necessary, the top leadership should seek outside operations expertise.

The model in this book will help you identify and overcome these obstacles. It starts with transformational change.

How to Build a World-Class-Performing Organization: A Model

> *Perfection consists not in doing extraordinary things, but in doing ordinary things extraordinarily well.*
> —Angelique Arnauld

Most people know they need to establish a road map in order to reach a desired destination. A model is the key to creating a road map well. It's a theory that indicates which factors are most critical or important. It also shows how these factors are related—that is, which factor or combination of factors causes other factors to change. Management's primary mission is to make organizations operate effectively. One effective way to achieve this is by using a model. Figure 1 outlines a model to build a high-performance world-class-performing organization.

Figure 1: A model to build a high-performance world-class-performing organization.

Transformation change is a difficult task. To bring about operational transformation is to bring about breakthrough change. Breakthrough change refers to disruptive initiatives that dramatically or profoundly affect the organization and the people in it. Seasoned executives know well—often by learning the hard way—that introducing and implementing breakthrough change is an uphill battle. You need to take a rigorous, action-oriented approach to make a complete transformation. Begin by translating your inspiring vision of the future into a workable, real-world plan. The more actions an organization takes, the more likely its transformation is to succeed.

No single transformation model guarantees success. However, the odds of success are greatly improved if you use a model and target leadership functions: make the transformation meaningful, model the desired mind-sets and behaviors, build a strong and committed team, and relentlessly pursue impact. Together, these can powerfully generate the energy needed to achieve a successful performance transformation.

Commit to achieve transformation. The CEO must commit to lead the transformation. The commitment should be very clear and in writing and most importantly shared with all employees. The CEO's commitment is the key to achieving operational transformation.

Set transformation goals. Dedicate time toward deciding what to change, what to change to, and how to make the change. This means perform an organizational performance risk assessment and come up with a written plan of action, including strategies involved and goals, and Wildly Important Goals (WIGs), which are critical for an organization's success.

Communicate. Communicate openly, continually, and across the organization. Spend more time communicating the change story and aligning the top-level team. Continually tell an engaging, tailored story about the changes that are underway. This has substantially more impact on the outcome than more programmatic elements, such as performance management or capability building. Communicate progress and increase your chances of success.

Lead by example. Leadership matters as much during a transformation as it does in the company's day-to-day work. It cannot be delegated to a project-management or central team. When senior leaders model the behavior changes they are asking employees to make, the transformations are more likely to be successful.

> *For things to change, I must change.*
> —Mahatma Gandhi

Engage employees. Choose the right people and empower them. Allocate enough employees and the right ones—that is, the high performers and active supporters (champions)—to work on the transformation. Focus on people, not the project. The long-term sustainability of a transformation requires companies to engage enthusiastic high-potential employees, equip them with skills, and hold them accountable for—as well as celebrate— their contributions to the effort.

Steadily improve execution. The key to improving execution is to methodically instill an execution culture and make it your organization's competitive advantage.

Create an organizational culture. Culture is everything. It is more important than strategy; some even say, "Culture eats strategy for lunch." Top leadership must make creating an appropriate culture the number-one priority. Organizations will succeed only if they create the right culture. All changes in organization are challenging, but perhaps the most daunting is changing the culture.

Continuously improve. Create an environment of continuous improvement so organizations can keep their performance from stagnating (or even regressing) once the transformation is achieved. By implementing continuous-improvement activities that enable the organization to look regularly for new and better ways to work, organizations can double their chance of successfully sustaining improvements after the transformation.

Deliberately reduce the cost of doing business. Continuously reduce product costs and improve operational efficiency and productivity throughout the organization. Create a well-oiled organization that operates at optimum cost.

Aim for customer focus/satisfaction. As a general goal, all of an organization's goals and actions should be customer focused. Customer (internal as well as external) satisfaction must be the prime objective.

Remember that transformation takes time, persistence, and continual effort through the following steps:

- ❖ Change processes.
- ❖ Change culture.
- ❖ Increase productivity.
- ❖ Create champions.
- ❖ Instill this culture: *Time is not a resource issue but is a priority issue.*
- ❖ Obtain additional employee support.

The return is manifold!

The methodology in this book was developed based on this model to build world-class-performing organizations.

Food for Thought

1. Does your organization use such a model? If yes, great. If not, why not?
2. What three transformational goals did your organization set last year?
3. Which three steps are critical for your organization? Are you doing anything about it?

CHAPTER 2

Ten-Step Methodology Outline

The ten steps of the methodology are broken up into three functional parts.

Part A concentrates on bringing change to people and leadership systems. It's about laying a solid foundation to bring operational transformation and contains the first four steps of the methodology, which are the most crucial and where you should focus 70 percent of your change efforts. The first step focuses on the CEO's commitment and is critical to the methodology's success. The next three steps are about instilling appropriate cultures to make transformation a success.

Parts B and C focus on key business processes to bring process change in your organization and are where you should focus the remaining 30 percent of your change efforts. Part B concentrates on steps 5 and 6 across two core business functions: execution and cost structure. Execution enables you to get things done and helps improve capability, while the cost structure helps improve profitability. Lastly, part C details the remaining four steps by providing a systematic approach to problem solving. These steps formalize management's primary responsibility, which is to solve problems.

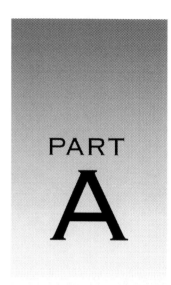

PART

A

LAY A SOLID FOUNDATION

Commitment and Culture

CHAPTER 3

Unwavering Relentless Commitment by CEO

Unless commitment is made, there are only
promises and hopes ... but no plans.
—Peter F. Drucker

The CEO helps a transformation succeed by communicating its significance, modeling the desired changes, building a strong team, and getting personally involved. Organizations cannot settle for incremental improvement; they must periodically undergo a performance transformation to get and stay on top—that is, they need to build and sustain the health of the organization.

Operational transformation does not happen by accident; it must be planned by the leadership in the organization. The journey begins with a power commitment by the CEO of the company to build a world-class-performing organization. A power commitment means that the organization is willing to devote precious time, spend money, and incur financial losses or forgo gains in adhering to its mission or purpose.

A power commitment means the CEO has to play a successful role in a transformation. He or she can play a successful role by doing the following:

1. Understand how to achieve operational transformation. This means comprehend and follow a proven operational transformation system. The next step is to realize that the CEO will likely need to

change himself or herself to act as a role model of desired mind-sets and behaviors.

2. Create a strong sense of purpose for your organization. Do this by working with your team to craft a mission or purpose statement and instill it into your company culture. Make the statement meaningful.

3. Gather a strong and committed leadership team. The CEO must make tough decisions about the ability and motivation of individual team members. The CEO's team can and should be a valuable asset in leading any transformation. Make an unwavering commitment both to and with your management team to achieve your transformation objectives. Ensure clearly visible signals that management is committed to operational transformation. For example, establish a monitoring system, and define the requirements for achieving operational transformation clearly.

4. Pursue/follow up relentlessly. Roll up your sleeves and get personally involved.

Take the time to personalize the story of your transformation. This can in turn significantly unlock more energy for the transformation. CEOs must invest great effort in visibly and vocally presenting the transformation story. You have to put your face in front of all the employees if you want them to follow you. Once the story is out, the CEO's role becomes one of constant reinforcement. Repeat, repeat, repeat the story and plans throughout the organization. The powerful way to reinforce the story is to highlight successes. Focusing on errors and mistakes can generate feelings of fatigue, blame, and resistance. Emphasize what works well and discuss how to get more out of those strengths to tap into creativity, passion, and the desire to succeed.

The power commitment needs to be an unwavering commitment. To make operational improvement efforts a success, the top leadership needs to make fundamental changes in themselves. They need to change their own mind-sets and the mind-sets of their teams. The CEO must dedicate at least 10 percent, on average, of company resources to the operational improvement initiative to build and sustain the long-term health of the organization.

Senior managers must act as role models. They must devise a system to measure culture change and then track it and drive it. All leaders must not be afraid to make the tough decisions.

Employees in an organization defend the status quo, so the leadership must follow a change management process. Performance-based reward systems can increase employee commitment. The organization must identify and address pervasive mind-sets at the outset to make the change effort a success. McKinsey research[3] indicates that if you do, you are four times more likely to succeed in organizational change efforts than are companies that overlook that stage of identifying the pervasive mind-sets.

Are you ready to make the power commitment to achieve transformation? If you are not quite sure, consider the following points:

1. What is the cost of inaction (lack of execution)? For example, the opportunity cost of time to market, cost structure (unnecessary costs, out-of-control expenses, etc.), carrying too much inventory or lack of inventory, undesired product cost, and so on.
2. Impact on employee morale of inaction or poor execution. For example, retention rate, cost of lost employees, plus cost of replacement.
3. Impact on productivity. For example, cost of unproductive employees, plus cost of low organizational productivity.
4. Risk of failures can be greatly reduced by building a world-class-performing organization.

Achieving transformation and building a world-class-performing organization is not inherently difficult. Unfortunately, business leaders rarely talk about it and even more rarely take steps to consciously build world-class-performing organizations. The main reason for this is that business leaders are busy with day-to-day activities and do not take time

---

[3] Nate Boaz and Erica Ariel Fox, "Change Leader, Change Thyself." *McKinsey Quarterly*, no. 4 (2014). Retrieved from McKinsey & Company.

to commit to creating world-class-performing organizations that are excellent, ethical, and enduring. If they make a commitment and get personally involved, the process can be straightforward, especially if they follow some kind of methodology. The methodology in this book may appear simple, but it represents complex ideas gleaned from many years of real-world learning. It is a comprehensive set of practical concepts that you can begin using immediately to create a more effective and productive organization.

Most of us start off pretty average. The difference between average people that create extraordinary results and those that do not is their level of commitment to something more. Are you ready to make this commitment?

In summary, it comes down to the company leadership to utilize the methodology discussed in this book effectively to gain a competitive edge. Top leadership has to make a commitment to apply all the principles for the betterment of the organization. The CEO will have to provide the leadership to communicate the commitment to all employees. Each group within the organization will have to provide leadership to instill the transformation culture in their employees to carry out the plan. If implemented successfully, your organization will get amazing results using the methodology discussed in this book.

How Can You Get Your Employees on Board with You?

If you broadcast your vision continually in all interactions, others will believe in it and act on it, and your leadership will turn it into reality. Great leaders convey the vision by persuasion. Communicate your laser-focus strategy consistently and thoroughly throughout the organization. Your organization's vision should be burned into the mind of every employee. Connect with your employees at three levels: (1) physical, (2) mental, and (3) emotional.

Are You a Leader?

Commitment is one quality that leaders exemplify. People will not believe the message if they don't believe in the messenger.
A leader is

- honest: Tell the truth.
- competent: Competency is an asset. It depreciates with time, so you need to develop yourself.
- inspirational: Be passionate and have enthusiasm.
- forward-looking: Share your vision.
- credible: Credibility is the foundation of leadership. Take a stand, and express your opinion.
- followed: Ensure you have followers.

Food for Thought

1. Are you leading your organization by example? How? Give example(s).
2. Are you personally following through? Describe the process.
3. Have you written down the transformation commitment clearly and explicitly? Have you shared it with all employees? Have you dedicated resources (time, energy, and money) to bring about the operational transformation?

CHAPTER 4

Create Organizational Alignment

My role is to try to get everyone in the organization aligned.
—Tony Hsieh, CEO, Zappos

Organization-wide alignment is very critical if you want to get the right things done and move your organization forward in the most effective and efficient way possible. Organizational alignment allows a business to maximize the power of all its resources. Everyone heads in the same direction. Employee engagement reaches its highest level. Organizations are able to maximize profits and results. Get everyone in the boat rowing the same direction. Organizational alignment occurs when the strategy is cascaded throughout the organization for development of plans and actions that support strategic intent. It requires discipline, commitment, and employee engagement to create alignment. Creating the right organizational alignment is not something that happens by chance, and often a great deal of effort and thought goes into the process. It will not occur on its own. As a leader, you must take the initiative to create organizational alignment.

It is equally important to align the organization on what not to do as it is to explain what to do. It is essential and at the same time very difficult to create a shared vision and alignment around the organization's strategic direction. Even the most brilliant business strategies will fail if the entire team is not aligned with the common goals and vision of the organization. Many organizations today operate at suboptimal performance levels, not because they lack competent employees or skills but because these organizations are not aligned.

Organizational dynamics is a system of internal customer and supplier relationships. When this relationship is in alignment, that is, the need of the customer is met by the supplier, the effectiveness of the organization is optimized. Thus, alignment is a must for achieving peak organizational performance. The challenge is how you go about aligning the organization.

This alignment can occur at many levels: company-wide, divisions, groups (e.g., department-department), and individuals (e.g., supervisor-subordinate). As a leader, it is necessary not only to tell people what they are expected to achieve but also to tell them how to go about it. Setting up clear expectations at every level is one of the simplest and most effective steps leaders can and should take to drive performance. It also means setting up systems, processes, policies, and rules to create alignment.

To begin the alignment process, you as a leader have to make sure employees understand three things:

1. What do you want them to do?
2. What's in it for them?
3. Are you (the leader) going to do it too?

The above three things will make people feel truly accountable for doing their part. In most organizations, the majority of employees are not engaged. True alignment will increase this number dramatically.

> The most important activities to create alignment are as follows:
>
> 1. Create a shared vision.
> 2. Mobilize teams to function as high-performing groups.
> 3. Spend the right amount of time to understand the organizational culture.

I have discovered that there are three areas to look at when creating alignment.

❖ "Government of the people, by the people, for the people"
❖ "Location, location, location"

If you want something to stick in someone's head, put it in a sequence of three.

Try to apply the rule of three. Divide a presentation into three parts. Introduce a product with three benefits. Give me three reasons to hire you! Use this methodology. It worked for Jefferson, it worked for Jobs, and it will work for you.

If your organization can pick and implement three major ideas, concepts, techniques, or tools from the methodology, it can start making significant progress. You can continue to do so (that is, once they are completed, go to the next three) until you feel your organization has achieved its operational transformation.

So employees will understand and retain, communication should have the following format:

❖ three key messages ---------------------------- maximum
❖ each with seven to twelve words -------------------- maximum
❖ three supporting facts ------------------------ maximum

The rule of three can be used to simplify a complex situation or matter. The rule of three when combined with the time principle becomes even more powerful. The time principle says that "time should not be viewed as a resource issue, but rather a priority issue, that is, figure out what is important for you or your organization. Managing time is about priorities, not resources." Once the top leadership makes an unwavering commitment to put these two principles into practice, the organization's progress will be almost unstoppable! This means the organization will significantly improve its execution. The use becomes pervasive and will create an adaptive organization. It will help motivate employees, and morale will increase as the progress will be visible. And as you may know, a motivated workforce can do wonders.

Remember—doing something isn't always better than doing nothing!

> ### In short, the rule of three
>
> 1. helps you set right priorities.
> 2. establishes a discipline to arrive at three—that is, learn to make complex things into simpler ones.
> 3. proves that ideas presented in threes are more interesting, enjoyable, and memorable.

Follow Three Rules to Build a World-Class-Performing Organization

The rule of three applies in building a world-class-performing organization. In order to achieve organizational excellence, a business needs to establish and strictly follow these three rules:

- ❖ Although change can start anywhere in an organization, it can only succeed if it is committed to by, led by, and modeled from the top.
- ❖ What gets measured, monitored, and rewarded is what matters.
- ❖ Unless operational excellence initiative is integrated into the organization's policies and practices, it will be redelegated to the wish list.

Follow and internalize the above rules. If you follow them, your chances of success will be manifold. These rules are business best practices but unfortunately are not followed by most organizations. These rules are a must to building world-class-performing organizations. The trick is to put a process or system in place for each element. The methodology shows how to do this.

Food for Thought

1. Does your organization realize the importance of the rule of three? Have you practiced it?
2. What rules are you using to build a strong organization?
3. Do all employees in your organization understand the time principle?

CHAPTER 6

Celebrate Successes to Keep Continually Improving

Celebrate what you want to see more of.
—Tom Peters

Change initiatives can be frustrating and take a long time to implement. It is therefore important to celebrate individual milestones along the way. If you want something to grow, pour champagne on it. Reinforcing successes will produce more successes. Systems of recognition and rewards help maintain a culture of motivation, unity, and satisfaction. Satisfied employees are more loyal and hardworking than their unsatisfied counterparts.

Rewards and recognition programs are underutilized in many organizations and can be a low-hanging fruit in your change efforts.

Benefits of a Rewards and Recognition Program

1. It allows you to communicate your message repeatedly.
2. It gives you the opportunity to instill the desired culture.
3. It recognizes and encourages champions within your organization.
4. It communicates progress. This links most closely with future successes.
5. It shows employees what to do and how to do it correctly.
6. What gets rewarded gets repeated.

How to Celebrate

There are several ways an organization can celebrate. It doesn't have to always be a big celebration; in fact, it is sometimes better if the smaller but more consistent methods are used because those things will positively impact the organization's culture. Consider the following ways to celebrate achievement.

1. Take time to say thank you. A genuine thank-you can go a long way toward leaving a more lasting impression—as well as a deeper entrenched respect.
2. Recognize successes at the start of a team meeting.
3. A pizza party and drinks after work go a long way.
4. Public displays of recognition in a company-wide or group or division meeting demonstrate respect.
5. Give out rewards that are appropriate to the individual or group.

Food for Thought

1. How often do you celebrate major milestones?
2. Can you describe your rewards and recognition program?
3. Do you use a performance-based rewards system?

PART
B

FOCUS ON TWO CORE
BUSINESS FUNCTIONS

CHAPTER 7

Master Execution and Focus Organizational Efforts

The two core functions in our methodology are execution and achieving the best possible cost structure. Learning how to manage tasks, priorities, and resources is critical for a business to improve productivity, so the execution step is subdivided into two sections: master execution and focus organizational efforts.

Master Execution

> *Execution is a systematic process of rigorously discussing hows and whats, tenaciously following through, and ensuring accountability.*
> —Larry Bossidy and Ram Charan in Execution[5]

Execution is a specific set of behaviors and techniques that companies need to master to win the game. Execution is a major responsibility of a business leader. It must be a core element of an organization's culture.

Simply speaking, execution means the discipline of getting things done and consequently getting the desired results. It also means turning goals into results and your vision into specific activities and tasks. Remember—knowledge is only potential power at best; execution is the power! Innovation is rewarded; execution is worshipped. It is clear that the ability to get things done is at the very core of exceptional performance.

---

[5]   Larry Bossidy and Ram Charan, *Execution: The Discipline of Getting Things Done* (Crown Business, New York City, June 2002).

You can have great strategies, master plans, and well-defined goals, but if you cannot execute, these things are useless and a waste of time, and chances are the company will fail.

Execution and Accountability

Mastering execution means: creating a culture of discipline and accountability. Discipline means training to act in accordance with rules. The word "discipline" implies it is difficult to do. Accountability is not punishment. It is a support system for winners. Accountability answers an essential question: Can I count on you? Accountability can be summed up with these points:

1. Clarification creates confidence. Confusion creates chaos.
2. Tracking does the heavy lifting of accountability. Consistent follow-up fosters accountability.
3. Goals make people accountable.

In order to make people truly accountable for doing their part, you have to make sure that your employees understand the following three things:

1. What do you want them to do?
2. What's in it for them?
3. Are you going to do it too?

Improving Execution

> Mastering execution means:
>
> 1. Have a laser-sharp focus and work hard.
> 2. Keep an eye on the future (do not mortgage your future)—survive and prosper.
> 3. Improve efficiencies and focus on cost savings.

Leading for execution is not a big deal; it's very straightforward. The main requirement is that you as a leader have to be deeply and passionately engaged in your organization and honest about its realities with others and yourself. You need to follow the "how to expose harsh realities" process discussed in chapter 10.

There are two schools of thought about the best way to improve execution.

One school emphasizes people: just put the right people in place, and the right things will get done. Some experts insist that the right people are hired, not made. Others think that the key is to improve executive performance through training and improve the average employee's performance through the creation of a culture of accountability. A second school of thought emphasizes process rather than people. Larry Bossidy is a proponent of this. The two schools are just two sides of the coin.

To improve execution, the theme should be "don't paint over problems instead of solving them." This means focus on exposing the harsh realities of your organization or the situation. If you do this, you will be on your way to making meaningful progress.

In order to master execution, you need to work on the following three major elements:

❖ Follow a system to instill an execution culture.
❖ Set three wildly important goals (WIGs) to undertake three major initiatives every year.
❖ Keep a scorecard/use an executive dashboard.

Follow a system to instill an execution structure. Based on my over thirty-five years of experience, I have developed an effective system to instill an execution culture. Once you implement all elements of the system, you will have created an execution culture, which will be your competitive advantage. Here are ten components of this system.

1. *Instill leadership skills.* One of the primary responsibilities of top leadership is to develop and groom leaders at all levels. The main difference between a leader and a manager is that a leader does the right things and a manager does things right. This means leaders

are effective (produce desired results) and managers are efficient (increase productivity).

There are hundreds of books written on leadership. It can be summarized that one needs to develop the following skills to become an effective leader. It is the responsibility of a leader to train, nurture, and prepare his or her staff so that they also become leaders.

Critical Leadership Skills

- Be visionary and become a strategist.
- Work closely with employees so they achieve peak performance.
- Possess excellent communications skills.
- Lead by example.
- Delegate tasks effectively.
- Master details.
- Possess the following organizational skills:
  - goal setting
  - problem solving
  - interpersonal skills

As discussed above, an organization needs leaders to produce desired results. However, organizations do not put enough efforts into developing leaders because it is not easy to do. The two major challenges are changing behavior and getting people to commit. Getting the commitment in the midst of the daily grind is not easy.

2. *Put an operations infrastructure in place.* You need to put an operations infrastructure in place to get things done right consistently throughout the organization. You will follow this process for each major initiative the organization undertakes. The process works as follows:

   1) Come up with a strategy for a given initiative.
   2) Put processes/systems in place to support the strategy.
   3) Set and monitor goals. Set, monitor, and track appropriate Key Performance Indicators (KPIs).

If the effort does not turn into results, something is wrong. If this is the case, look into the following:

- the objectives, targets, and strategies that were set
- the actions being pursued
- the people involved

Once you look into the above points, revisit the three steps of operations infrastructure and make necessary adjustments.

3. *Employ a unique management style.* Based on my over thirty-five years of experience, I have developed a unique management technique to produce desired results. This technique encompasses seven disciplines of management discussed in chapter 12 under step 10: Have a Management System in Place. It has three main steps.

   1) *Set Goals:* We will talk more about how to go about setting and achieving goals in chapter 9 under step 7. While establishing goals, focus on setting learning goals, not just output goals.
   2) *Focus:* Focus means two things:
      First, it means
      Follow
      One
      Course
      Until
      Successful.
      Secondly, it means apply the Pareto principle. This principle, named after economist Vilfredo Pareto, specifies an unequal relationship between inputs and outputs. The principle states that, for many phenomena, 20 percent of invested input is responsible for 80 percent of the results obtained. For example, 20 percent of customers bring in 80 percent of the revenue. Here is your opportunity to put the power of the rule of three to work! Since no organization has unlimited resources, it is very important that this step is strictly followed

to increase productivity and consequently get more things done in a given time. We will discuss a detailed process to focus the organization's efforts, that is, how to set priorities, in chapter 7.

3) *Track and Drive:* Tracking is your mechanism for communicating clearly and unambiguously the performance that is occurring at the enterprise, business unit, department, and individual levels. The best employees appreciate the importance of tracking. If you have the right people on your team, peer pressure is a powerful accountability force.

To track means to measure where you are and where you want to go. Measure things that are most important to you. If you want to improve something, you have to measure it. Here you want to keep track of major KPIs to improve your performance. For example, you may want to establish KPIs related to on-time delivery performance, product yields, inventory, customer returns, and outgoing quality.

Remember—when progress is measured, progress improves. When progress is measured and reported, improvement accelerates.

Tracking increases accountability. Great people want to see progress. Limit metrics to three items and make tracking visible. Why do we want to track?

- to eliminate surprises and improve decision making
- to minimize subjectivity and emotion in addressing performance
- to provide a performance scorecard (which we will discuss in detail later in this chapter)

Driving means identifying obstacles and problems that prevent you from achieving the desired performance and taking actions. Since 85 percent of the problems are system-, process-, or communications-related, you want to identify process- or system-related problems and generate plans to fix them. Focus on fixing such problems rather than fixing people!

4. Establish a change management process.

> *Change is the law of life. And those who look only to the*
> *past or present are certain to miss the future.*
> —John F. Kennedy

Why do you want to establish a solid change management process in your organization?

Thirty years of research by leadership guru Dr. John Kotter have proven that 70 percent of all major change efforts in organizations fail.[6]

The change management process means how to handle change, for example, how to initiate and implement a major initiative. There are two change drivers: opportunity and pain. Most of the time, it is pain that drives change. In most cases, change is met with resistance. The trick is to figure out how to overcome the resistance to change. If you pursue the following process, you will have a very high probability to overcome the resistance to change and will be able to implement the change successfully.

Where does the resistance come from?

- lack of information
- fear
- people trying to control the situation

Pursue the following process to increase the probability of overcoming the resistance:

Change Management Process

1) Keep employees informed of the change and avoid surprises completely. To get buy-in from unwilling employees, it will serve you well to begin by explaining to them the reasons behind the change. This step is important if you are to motivate any unwilling staff members. It is important that you communicate your change

---

[6] Dr. John Kotter, *The 8-Step Process for Leading Change.* (Harvard Business School Press, Brighton, 1996).

program (as much of it as is possible) on a regular and timely basis. No one likes to be surprised.

2) Get employees involved in generating action items, making decisions, and implementing the change. Give them tools to manage change and time to actually solve problems. Involve a variety of employees in the planning, decision making, and monitoring stages of the change strategy. By including members across the organizational hierarchy, you are more likely to gain their support/buy-in and less likely to surprise anyone.

3) Create champions at all levels who support the change wholeheartedly. Find individuals throughout the organization who can serve as champions of your change program. These individuals carry influence among other staff members; their ability to convince others of the merits of the desired change strategies makes them effective proponents of the program.

In order to increase your chances of overcoming resistance to change, you must

- embed things into processes. That is, change management practices and techniques must be built in in everything you do.
- realize the fact that a workforce that is flexible, open-minded, and interested in learning is far better than a workforce that is determined to keep doing things the old way.
- encourage resistance to change. Why?
  - Resistance is a driving force. The act of resisting, in itself, is a tremendous source of energy.
  - When people resist, it is your opportunity to show that you are hearing them.
  - If you yourself are afraid of resistance triggers, you will meet even stronger resistance from your people. Instead, if you encourage resistance as a natural process to accompany change, compassionately showing that you hear people's fears, your stakeholders will be a lot more inclined to trust you rather than to oppose you.

5. *Follow an effective communication process.* There is a process for effective communication. The steps below delineate this process:

   a) Repeat, repeat, repeat your message to get it across. You need to communicate seven times in seven different ways to stick in people's minds.
   b) Listen to understand. Listening increases likability, and likability leads to trust. Listening to understand means you don't hear just to respond, but you try to understand the other person's point of view and what he or she is after.
   c) Explain the importance and show the benefits of doing something. In order to get things done, you need to explain *why* you want the other person to do something. Once the person understands the importance, he or she will be more inclined or convinced to do the task.

Again, in order to get things done satisfactorily, you must communicate how the organization or a group or a person will benefit once the task is completed.

6. *Understand team challenges.* A team is not a group of people who work together. A team is a group of people who trust each other and share expertise. Why is it difficult to form an effective team? Here are the challenges when it comes to teams:

   • Absence of Trust. To increase trust, listen to understand. Listening increases likability, and likability leads to trust. Also, you must make and keep your promises in order to increase trust.
   • Fear of Conflict. Team members fear conflict because many times emotions are involved. One of my managers told me, "Facts are our friends." When you use facts, you can get emotions out and reduce the chances of conflict.
   • Avoidance of Commitment. When you have team interests in mind, you should not hesitate to make commitments. Always

think about what is good for the team and do your part, for example, make the appropriate commitment.

- Lack of Accountability. Once the team members trust each other and make commitments, each member will feel accountable.
- Inattention to Results. A team must have goals. Teams cannot function without goals.

7. *Follow a corporate strategic continuous improvement system; constantly determine what to change, what to change to, and how to make the change.*

One of the most difficult situations any organization faces is to determine what needs to be changed. This is so because it is harder to see the problem than to solve it. How can you see the problem? One of the best ways to do this is to analyze where you are, where you want to go, and how you want to get there. This means you need to do gap analysis. Your vision will tell you where you want to go. In order to find out where you are, you need to carry out performance risk assessment for your organization. Once you compare your findings with the vision, you will know what needs to be done—that is, what and how to close the gap. Based on this, the next step is to generate three major initiatives the organization should undertake. These initiatives will show you what to change, what to change to, and how to make the change. The initiatives will become three WIGs for the year. Then you need to track and drive these initiatives until they are completed.

You need to repeat the whole cycle periodically.

8. *Pursue a system to develop and retain employees.* Since employees are the biggest asset for any organization, top leadership should spend enough time and resources to develop their employees. Here is how you can do just that:

mployees to speak frankly with their managers without fear
repercussions.

mmunity Involvement: By providing community services,
organization shows that it is a good corporate citizen.
loyees appreciate working for such organizations.

eam-building process. Teams are formed to pool the
experience, skills, and expertise of each individual.
ilding process has nine steps:

rtise.
ssion/objective/goal for the team.
members accountable; discuss the consequences
r not achieving the goal.
nent.
nable team members.
s.

g steps. As your company moves toward
, job performance will need to change.

llent Job Performance

or and establish goals for yourself
, etc.). Always try your best to

ded, to accomplish urgent tasks.
respect of your supervisor and

ions/suggestions to improve
Include your recommended
may raise awareness about

A System t

1. Mind-set: realize
   Be sympathetic
   ideas and des'
2. Trust and
   importar
3. Comm
4. Find
5. De

6.

e
of
c) Co
an
Emp

9. Follow a
knowledge,
The team-bu

1) Share expe
2) Define a m
3) Make team
   of achieving
4) Gain commit
5) Empower and
6) Monitor progres
7) Coach.
8) Reinforce.
9) Provide feedback.

10. Job performance-enhancir
    its new objectives, at time

How to Achieve Exc

a) Work with your supervis
   (weekly, quarterly, annua
   accomplish the goals.
b) Put in extra effort, when nee
c) Be a team player. Gain the
   colleagues.
d) Come up with recommendat
   the way your company operates.
   solution(s) with any problem you

44

e) Take an initiative in everything you do. Be proactive rather than reactive. Respond to any request within twenty-four hours (for the first response).

f) Focus on fixing systems/processes for continuous improvement rather than carrying out temporary fixes.

g) Identify your strengths and weaknesses. Take full advantage of your strengths and continuously work on areas needing improvement.

h) Keep your supervisor and others informed of your major activities verbally as and when needed, and also via e-mail, meetings, written reports, and so on.

i) When you call a meeting, make sure that you publish the agenda before the meeting and the action items after the meeting. Always show up at the meeting on time.

j) Bring a sense of humor to work. Smile, smile, smile.

Set three wildly important goals to undertake three major initiatives every year. What is a wildly important goal (WIG)? A WIG is a goal that can make all the difference in your organization. It is similar to what Jim Collins and Jerry Porras call in their book *Built to Last*[7] a BHAG (big hairy audacious goal). You will be spending a dedicated amount of time, energy, and efforts on it, the estimated 15 to 20 percent that is not used up in tactical matters. You will identify an area of improvement that will have the greatest impact. This goal should set the new performance standard for your organization. You should set no more than one goal each for the three major business functions: execution, cost structure, and problem solving. The WIG will be the key to sustaining the health of the organization.

When you have three WIGs instead of a dozen we-really-hope goals, the effect on morale is dramatic. This is one of the ways to boost the morale of your team and provide an environment for employees to get motivated and excited.

---

[7] Jerry Porras and James Collins, *Built to Last: Successful Habits of Visionary Companies* (New York City: William Collins, 1994).

Pursue the following process to set three WIGs:

1. Determine what to change.
2. Determine what to change to.
3. Determine how to make the change.

1) *Determine what to change: How to identify three major corporate initiatives.* Every year in the last quarter, carry out an organizational evaluation to identify the areas that need the most improvement and, if improved, will have the greatest impact on performance results.

   Once you follow the above process, the result will be the areas that need to be addressed by major corporate initiatives.

2) *Determine what to change to.* Refer to the corporate problem-solving model in chapter 11 and use the five-questions approach to get to what to change to.

   Five-Question Structure to Get to the Bottom of the Issue

   1) What is the best thing that happened to our organization, or what is working for us?
   2) What makes that the best thing or what makes that work?
   3) What would be ideal for our organization? (Future vision.)
   4) What is not quite right yet? (Get to the problem.)
   5) How can we close the gap? (What resources or knowledge will we need?)

3) *Determine how to make the change.* You need to follow the how to "put an operations infrastructure in place" process discussed in chapter 9 to make the change as follows:

   - Come up with a strategy for a given initiative.
   - Put in place systems and/or processes to support the strategy.
   - Set goals (set three WIGs based on the SMART goals model): who is going to do what and when?

- Monitor (weekly WIG meeting no longer than twenty to thirty minutes, focusing on lagging and leading indicators)
- Feedback (adjust goals, change strategy and/or system/process as appropriate)

Keep a scorecard/use an executive dashboard. Imagine trying to fly an airplane across the country with a cockpit that had no dashboard, no gauges, and no indicator lights. You might get it off the ground, but without the ability to measure performance, the chances of getting to where you want to go are slim to none. For business success, it takes performance management to get you where you want to go. Today, the performance scorecard is a performance measurement system that helps companies pursue their key success factors. The scorecard uses both internal and external benchmarking and employs a relevant cascading method of performance goal setting. Achievements are acknowledged and celebrated on a real-time basis, not during the traditional annual review.

Most organizations don't keep score or understand what to keep score of. They are not clear on how to measure their successes and failures. They do not understand and comprehend the importance of scorekeeping. A robust set of organizational metrics allows executives to monitor a company's performance and health. What's needed is a manageable number of metrics that strike a balance among different areas of the business and are linked directly to whatever drives its value. A list of typical indicators for a high-tech company is presented shortly.

You need a scorecard for your employees to know the score at all times, so that they can tell whether or not they are winning. Scorecards are great at keeping employees engaged. If the KPIs are not kept on a visual scorecard, they will disappear into the whirlwind. Employees disengage when they don't know the score. When KPIs are tracked regularly, employees are actively involved. Great teams know, at every moment, whether or not they are winning. They must know; otherwise, they don't know what they have to do to win the game. An effective scorecard tells the team where they are and where they should be. This information is essential to the team to solve problems and make timely decisions.

Once employees can see the score, the level of play rises, and now they want to win.

A Scorecard

1. A performance scorecard is a graphical representation of progress over time of some entity, such as an enterprise, an employee, or a business unit, toward some specified goal(s). The integral concepts of scorecards are targets and key performance indicators (KPIs). KPIs are metrics used to evaluate factors that are critical to the success of an organization. Targets are specific goals for those indicators.

2. An executive dashboard is a visual representation, such as an Excel spreadsheet, that gives executives a quick and easy way to view their company's performance in real time. It displays the KPIs that corporate officers need to effectively run an enterprise.

3. Business dashboards can be a powerful tool for executives because they summarize complex information and present it in an easily digestible way.

There are three key components of an effective scorecard:

1. Keep it simple and make it easily visible.
2. Include key leading and lagging indicators.
3. An effective scorecard shows, within a few seconds, whether you are winning or losing.

There are two types of key performance indicators that a business needs to track periodically to make meaningful progress. They are lagging and leading indicators.

Lagging indicators tell you if you have achieved the desired results based on your goals. They are called lagging indicators because by the time you get the data, the result has already happened. A leading indicator tells you if you are likely to achieve the goal. The beauty of leading indicators is that they are predictive, meaning that if the leading indicator changes, you can anticipate that the lagging indicator will also change. The leading indicator is also controllable; it can be controlled by the team.

Lagging indicators provide a benchmark to determine month-to-month improvement but do not help make an actual improvement. They by themselves will not produce significant results, but when combined with leading indicators, they will produce meaningful and significant results.

Leading indicators are much more difficult to determine than lagging indicators. The major challenge for the organization is to come up with effective leading indicators. Coming up with the right leading indicators is really about helping everyone see themselves as strategic business partners and engaging them in conversation about what can be done better or differently to achieve the desired results, such as WIGs. Acting on leading indicators is necessary to achieve excellent performance. However, it is also the single most difficult aspect of instilling this discipline in your team. The reason is that the leading indicators are predictive and do not provide a guarantee of success. This not only makes it difficult to decide which leading indicators to use; it also tends to cause heated debate as to the validity of the measure at all. To fuel the debate further, leading indicators frequently require an investment to implement an initiative prior to a result being seen by a lagging indicator.

Just as a simple lever can move a big rock, a good leading indicator provides powerful leverage. Organizations must spend time and effort to come up with good effective leading indicators to produce significant results. Begin by brainstorming possible leading indicators and narrow your focus to a few leading indicators that will permit strong leverage.

A combination of leading and lagging indicators results in enhanced business performance overall. For example, preventive maintenance of equipment is a leading indicator of equipment uptime. When developing a business performance management strategy and system, it is always a good practice to use a combination of leading and lagging indicators. The reason for this is obvious: a lagging indicator without a leading indicator will give no indication as to how likely it is that a result will be achieved and will provide no early warnings about tracking toward a strategic goal. In short, leading indicators are performance drivers, and lagging indicators are outcome measures. The leading indicator is what the team can affect. The lagging indicator is the result they want. Nothing affects morale and engagement more powerfully than when a person feels he or she is winning.

When leading and lagging indicators are tracked and driven regularly, outstanding results are produced.

A List of Typical Indicators for a High-Tech Company
(This list can be used for any industry.)

Cost-Related Indicators

- gross profit margin (GPM) of 80 percent revenue products
- inventory—WIP, FGS, suppliers
- operating expense as a percentage of revenue
- product yields
- yield and purchase price variances
- employee/organizational productivity
- capital expense as a percentage of revenue

Quality-Related Indicators

- outgoing product quality
- customer returns
- customer surveys
- manufacturing process control capability index (Cpk's) [e.g., assembly Cpk]
- manufacturing parameter trends (e.g., PCM, ET)
- reliability

New Product-Related Indicators

- new product introduction status
- productization (how to manufacture high-yielding product) meeting
- product qualification status
- product characterization status

Manufacturing-Related Indicators

- on-time delivery (OTD) performance
- on-time performance of suppliers
- rolling forecast
- cycle times (e.g., fab, assembly, test)
- manufacturing/test productivity
- equipment uptime and utilization

Miscellaneous Indicators

- accountability matrix
- culture tracking matrix

Food for Thought

1. Are there any items in your ten-step execution structure that you can improve?
2. Do you need to change the way you communicate?
3. How effective is your communication? How will you measure it?

Focus Organizational Efforts

Focus is the hidden driver of excellence. Focus means handling multiple tasks and priorities effectively to increase productivity. It also means addressing the most common corporate issue: using resources effectively. In order to achieve operational excellence, one of the first things the top leadership has to do is to make sure that the organization's efforts are focused. These can be company efforts, department efforts, or individual efforts.

How to keep focus:

- persistence, persistence, persistence
- relentless communication
- play as though you are behind.

To begin with, in order to focus, use two broad-based strategies:

1. Deflect: ignore unnecessary stuff.
2. Use 3-D techniques:

   a) Delegate.
   b) Delay → Decide what to delay → Use filters.
   c) Delete → Is it necessary?

A Seven-Step Process

Pursue the following "How to Focus" process to greatly increase your organization's productivity. Top leadership will have to make this process a part of your organization's execution culture.

1. *Remember—time is not a resource issue; it is a priority issue.* Time should not be viewed as a resource issue but rather a priority issue. Managing time is about priorities, not resources. Each individual gets almost the same amount of time to get things done. Then how come some individuals are more effective and efficient than most

others? One of the answers is that they know how to manage their time. This means they follow knowingly or unknowingly some kind of a process similar to the one described here.

2. *Are these the "right" things to do?* First, make a list of things to do by organization, department, or individual. Then review the list and decide if these are the right things to do by asking the following questions:

   a) Does the given item support the company vision/mission?
   b) Does it take care of employees?
   c) Does it take care of your customers? (If you take care of your employees first, they will take care of your customers.)
   d) Does it take care of your organization (support other departments, do what's good for the organization, etc.)?

After answering the above questions, generate a list of "right" things to do.

3. *Apply the Pareto (80/20) Principle to set priorities.* The next step is to set priorities that correspond to the list generated in item 2 above. This means applying the Pareto or 80/20 Principle. (We discussed this principle earlier in the book in chapter 6.) In short, the way the principle works is to get a bigger bang for your buck, that is, identify items of importance that will have a major impact on the outcome. For example, 80 percent of revenue comes from 20 percent of customers. So if you want to address customer issues, make sure you take care of these 20 percent customers first.

After following this process, generate a list of "important" things to do from the list of "right" things to do generated in item 2 above.

Another tool for establishing priorities is Stephen Covey's Four-Quadrant Theory,[8] where you build a 2 x 2 grid, labeling the two columns as Urgent and Not Urgent, and the rows as Important and Not Important, and you proceed to fill out the quadrants.

---

[8] Stephen Covey, *The 7 Habits of Highly Effective People* (New York City: Free Press, 1989).

4. *Take the list from the above item and convert it into goals using the SMART goals model*, which is discussed in detail in chapter 9.

5. *Persevere, persevere, persevere.* To persevere means to continuously and consistently follow up.

6. *Track and drive.* Once the goals list is generated, track it and drive it periodically. To track means to find out where you are and where you want to go. To drive means to identify process- and/or system-related issues and fix them.

7. *Relentless communication.* Relentless communication in one or more of the following forms will help track and drive issues.

   a) staff meeting
   b) goals review meeting
   c) task force meeting
   d) periodic communications meeting
   e) 1:1 meeting
   f) operations review meeting

Remember—if you have more than three priorities at a time, you don't have any priority.

Food for Thought

1. What are your top three priorities for next year?
2. Do your activities support these priorities?
3. Have you used/followed Steven Covey's Four-Quadrant Theory?

CHAPTER 8

Achieve the Best Possible Cost Structure

Every company seeking profitable, sustainable growth must have a sound cost structure. In the long term, it is essential for any competitive business to stay competitive through achieving continuous cost reductions that enable costs to reach a level that is below the average of the company's competitors. It is not necessary to become the lowest cost provider, but it is necessary to be one of the lower cost suppliers. To stay competitive through continuous cost reductions, organizations should use some kind of methodology such as the one discussed in this chapter, the gross profit margin improvement system. True profitability comes when a company is able to continuously reduce the costs of producing and supplying products and services, while adjusting for inflation and other economic effects.

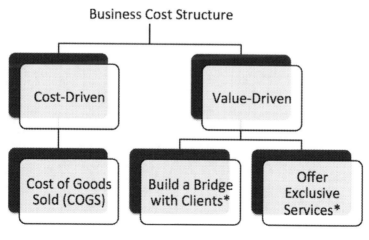

*Operational Excellence-Related

The methodology to achieve the best cost structure discussed in this chapter emphasizes reducing COGS to improve gross profit margin and achieve operational excellence. Operational excellence is about efficiency, effectiveness, and doing the right things right the first time.

Lowering cost by one dollar has a greater impact on the bottom line than increasing the revenue by one dollar because revenue always comes with an associated cost. Having a low cost structure is a strong competitive advantage. If you do not understand your cost structure, you are at a competitive disadvantage. Remember that cost savings are not a onetime effort; they must become part of the corporate culture—an ongoing quest for continuous improvement. To be successful, cost cutting must become a way of life.

The best cost structure means an organization is running at a minimum or optimum cost. It also means the organization has the lowest possible cost of doing a business. In short, achieving the best cost structure means minimizing the total cost of doing business and consequently increasing profitability, day in and day out. The world-class-performing organization that is most effective and efficient will operate consistently at minimum cost. Such an organization will have the following characteristics:

Characteristics of an Organization with the Best Cost Structure

- Human interactions and relationships are optimized.
- It operates at optimized man, machine, and method productivity.
- The organization has the lowest possible product cost, including quality cost. Quality cost is the cost required to perform inspections, repairs, etc.

The characteristics of an organization with the best cost structure are ideal, but most organizations have to change to acquire all three of those characteristics. There are challenges to building an organization with such characteristics.

Challenges to Building an Organization with the Best Cost Structure

- Reduce product cost faster than falling ASPs (Average Selling Price).
- Improve operational efficiency.
- Establish effective processes/systems to improve employee and organizational productivity.

Model to Achieve the Best Possible Cost Structure

The methodology offers a model to achieve the best possible cost structure to meet the above challenges. I developed this model after working for eleven high-tech companies, watching successful companies, and discerning what they did and did not do to manage cost. The model has three main parts, listed below, with multiple steps in each.

Part 1: Gross Profit Margin Improvement System

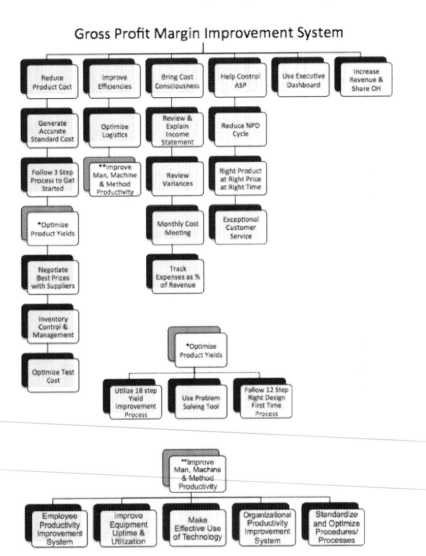

Figure 2: A visual representation of the gross profit margin improvement system.

Figure 2 is a visual representation of the gross profit margin improvement system. Here is a breakdown of the process of increasing GPM in bite-size chunks that are doable and produce visible results.

The Top Three Strategies of a GPM Improvement System

- Reduce product cost, including quality cost.
- Improve company-wide efficiency.
- Foster cost consciousness.

Strategy 1: Reduce Product Cost. There are several aspects to product cost. Let's look at seven methods to reduce the cost.

1. *Generate accurate standard cost:* It is crucial that the organization generates an accurate standard cost because future critical business decisions will be made based on it. The operations and cost accounting groups should work very closely and should spend a considerable amount of time to generate the standard cost. They also need to update it whenever any cost factor changes. The most important cost factors are material cost, test costs (e.g., wafer test and final test for a semiconductor company), assembly cost, and overhead costs. How you calculate overhead cost will be very critical, as it will have an impact on the gross margin.

2. *Follow a three-step process to get started:* This step is necessary to generate the future cost reduction game plan. The first step is to get an ASP road map for a few years from marketing for a given new product. Based on the expected gross profit margin and ASP, generate a cost road map (see the graph below). The last step is to generate a game plan for each cost point. This means that the operations group needs to come up with a cost reduction plan for each cost point and execute these plans.

It has been my experience that this essential process is not followed by many organizations.

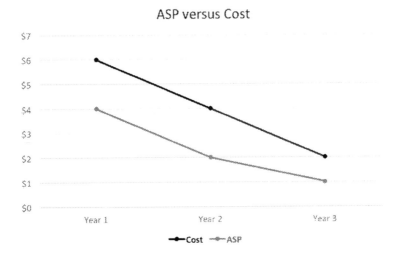

ASP versus Cost

3. *Optimize product yield:* Even though this section is based on the author's experience with the semiconductor industry, most of the things discussed below are applicable to any industry. The section contains several lists in three main sections, so readers are requested to pay close attention to get the most out of these sections. For example, read each subsection carefully to discern and interpret the information before you go to the next subsection.

Section I: Utilize an Eighteen-Step Yield Management System

Process and System-Related Strategies
1. Have a yield database.
2. Create a problem/solution database.
3. Have a yield-management software.
4. Have access to failure analysis tools.

Drive the following issues:
5. Emphasize right design first time (RDFT) requirements.
6. Follow wafer sort and final test yield improvement guidelines.

Establish a yield improvement culture:
7. Provide leadership and instill a continuous improvement culture.
8. Hold weekly yield meetings; review yield trends and drive issues.

9. Report yields monthly.
10. Take yield loss as early as possible.

Monitor the following:
11. ET (PCM) and in-line monitor Cpk's.
12. Defect density and ET parameter trends.
13. Yield variances.

Miscellaneous Strategies:
14. Set yield goals for product engineers.
15. Use the unique management style to drive issues.
16. Utilize the six sigma-based problem-solving tool.
17. Make sure the test pattern matches product design parameters.
18. Establish effective communications channels with foundries.

Section II: Follow a Twelve-Step Right Design First Time Process

1. Address design for manufacturing (DFM) issues.
2. Address design for test (DFT) issues.
3. Simulate the circuit over voltages and supplies.
4. Simulate at system level (whole circuit).
5. Use latest given technology process files for spice models.
6. Resolve spec differences between spice model limits and ET/PCM test limits.
7. Use checks and balance system in design engineering group.
8. Optimize/standardize design methodologies.
9. Match test pattern with actual design.
10. Use state-of-the-art design and layout tools.
11. Establish NPI (new product introduction) process.
12. Hold productization meetings.

Section III: Problem-Solving Tool (Paynter Chart)

This tool is extensively discussed in chapter 11 under step 9 of the methodology.

4. Negotiate best prices with suppliers: Price reduction is one way you can get the best price, but you can also build a partnership with your suppliers.

Price Reduction Strategies

1. Find out if the supplier is price gouging
2. Negotiate preproduction pricing
3. Negotiate production or volume pricing
4. Sell a company vision
5. If appropriate, negotiate spot pricing
6. If appropriate, negotiate die-based pricing
7. Find out industry pricing
8. Obtain CEO/BOD support
9. Develop an alternate source
10. Look for high-quality, hungry suppliers

Follow the following strategies to build outstanding supplier relationships:

Partnership Building Strategies

1. Approach each relationship with a win/win attitude. The goal is how to make each other successful. No politics, no surprises.
2. Negotiate in good faith in a totally open fashion.
3. Share business plans and future opportunities openly.
4. Be a good customer. Provide a believable, accurate forecast.
5. Establish communications channels.
6. Visit your suppliers as and when necessary.
7. Pick suppliers that are number one in their field/reputation.
8. Consider this: do they add value other than cost?
9. Select suppliers that are in the proximity of the customers.

5. *Utilize a nineteen-step inventory management and control system:* By carefully managing and controlling inventory, organizations can reduce cost. Use the following strategies to help reduce product cost:

Process- and System-Related Strategies
1. Select and implement Excel/MRP/ERP system.
2. Use JIT, Kanban, or similar inventory control system.

3. Establish a forecast planning process.
4. Use an on-the-fly yield forecast.

Drive the following issues:
5. Improve on-time delivery (OTD) performance.
6. Manage the new product introduction (NPI) process effectively.
7. Manage the end-of-life (EOL) process effectively.
8. Reduce fab, assembly, and test cycle times.
9. Improve test floor productivity.

Establish an inventory management and control culture:
10. Track progress weekly.
11. Report monthly.
12. Consider inventory ownership (no one group owns inventory).
13. Make suppliers partners.

Monitor the following:
14. Suppliers' performance
15. Inventory, tracked as a KPI.

Miscellaneous Strategies:
16. Come up with corporate inventory technique.
17. Use bottom-up forecast when appropriate.
18. Work hard to come up with accurate forecast.
19. Improve logistics (supply chain design).

6. *Optimize test cost:* Since all products need testing and the test cost is one of the major cost components, a significant amount of effort needs to be spent in reducing and optimizing test cost.

Test Cost Reduction Strategies

1. Address DFT issues with design engineering.
2. Optimize test program.
3. Characterize products and optimize test flows.
4. Improve equipment uptime and utilization.
5. Standardize software and hardware development.

6. Migrate to cheaper tester platform.
7. Use offshore testing.
8. Use parallel testing (WS & FT).

7. *Build quality and reliability in the product:* The best way to build quality and reliability in the product is to follow the Twelve-Step Right Design First Time Process given above and to monitor the reliability of the product on an ongoing basis.

Strategy 2: Improve Company-Wide Efficiency. Whenever you improve company-wide efficiency, you will improve productivity and hence will reduce the cost of doing business. This means improved profitability. This strategy has two parts:

1) Improve man, machine, and method productivity.
2) Optimize supply chain logistics.

1). Improve man, machine, and method productivity.

- Utilize employee productivity improvement system.
- Improve equipment uptime and utilization.
- Use organizational productivity improvement system.
- Standardize and optimize procedures and processes.
- Make effective use of technology.

2). Optimize supply chain logistics.
In order to reduce expenses and to be more responsive to the customer, a significant effort should be spent and focused to come up with a supply chain logistics strategy and design.

Strategy 3: Foster Cost Consciousness. To keep cost in line and achieve your goals for profitability, you need to make your people aware of the cost and its consequences. Do the following:

1. Review and explain income statement.
2. Hold monthly cost review meeting (mfg. & cost accounting).

3. Track expenses as a percentage of revenue.
4. Review yield, purchase price, and other variances.

Strategy 4: Help Control ASP. The ASP is more or less determined by the market. However, an organization can do the following things to command better ASP than its competitors:

1. Provide exceptional customer service.
2. Reduce time to market by reducing new product development cycle.
3. Ship quality products: right product at right time at right price!

Strategy 5: Use Performance Scorecard/Executive Dashboard. This topic is extensively discussed in chapter 6 under Step 5A: Master Execution.

Strategy 6: Increase Revenue and Share Overhead Expenses. Since most of the overhead expenses are fixed, it's a good idea to increase revenue to improve gross profit margin (GPM). This is a fundamental business strategy to improve GPM.

Part 2: Increase Organizational Productivity

The first principle to follow to improve organizational productivity is to create a culture of accountability and discipline. If employees are disciplined and accountable, they will be motivated and will produce the most.

The second principle is to systematize everything an organization does.

The third principle to increase organizational productivity is to make sure that the top leadership has made an unwavering commitment to bring about operational transformation and to make continuous improvement in everything the company does.

In addition to adhering to those three principles, you'll also need to take the following three approaches to increase organizational productivity.

Approaches to Improve Organizational Productivity

1. Leadership and cultural techniques
2. Management techniques
3. Miscellaneous techniques

Leadership and cultural techniques. A high-performance culture is a productive culture. Leadership can create that culture if it is lacking, by using the following techniques:

a) Have a well-defined vision and mission for the organization.
b) If you set habits, that will shift your thinking. Do this by instilling the appropriate cultures, especially the culture of discipline and accountability. Establish effective communications channels.
c) Create organizational alignment.
d) Use methodology and models.
e) Systematize: set up effective systems and processes for major business functions.
f) Harness the power of all employees.

Management techniques. Leaders should ensure that managers are actively involved in the process and are positively impacting the culture. The following techniques can help leaders accomplish this:

a) Focus/do the right things—that is, set priorities accordingly.
b) Take advantage of the power of the rule of three.
c) Improve operational efficiency.
d) Utilize results-oriented management style.
e) Establish effective communications channels.
f) Improve planning.
g) Create and exercise close supervision.
h) Undertake three initiatives (WIGs) every year.
i) Identify champions and create leaders at all levels.

Miscellaneous techniques. Utilize the simple yet powerful six sigma-based problem-solving tool discussed in chapter 11 under step 9.

a) Use Statistical Process Control (SPC) as appropriate.
b) Provide training to all employees.
c) Select and effectively use technology.
d) Reduce waste—that is, improve yield.
e) Follow the following "Process" productivity improvement system:

  1) Standardize the process.
  2) Optimize the process.
  3) Compare against the best case.
  4) Make sure each process step adds value—that is, eliminate nonvalue steps.

Part 3: Improve Operational Efficiency

Improving operational efficiency means developing systems and processes for talent retention and management to save time and resources and ultimately save on the cost of labor. It means creating an environment where employees are motivated. The talent management system focuses on identifying, selecting, hiring, developing, and retaining the talent required to deliver your competence and strategy. The talent management system includes behavioral science, a proven selection and hiring process (predicting performance), and team development (enhancing performance).

Follow the ten-step process described below to improve operational efficiency. These are the same steps that we discussed when we talked about a system to develop employees in part A of the methodology.

The top three steps are as follows:

1. Mind-Set: Realize the fact that employees are your biggest asset. Be sympathetic (look for positives) and be empathetic to their ideas and desires.
2. Trust and value your employees. Make them feel genuinely important.
3. Communicate, communicate, communicate; listen to them.

The other seven steps are as follows:

4. Find out what they want and show them how to get it.
5. Delegate tasks. Ask questions to guide employees to think through the issues and come up with their own solutions.
6. Make employees goals-oriented. Challenge them to motivate them.
7. Employ recognition—give awards and rewards, send notes, and so on.
8. Harvest creativity: Allow for mistakes and failures but match freedom with stiff expectations and high standards.
9. Focus on fixing systems and processes rather than fixing people.
10. Provide tools/resources/job-related training as and when needed.

In summary, follow the E's to motivate your employees:

1. Example—lead by example. For example, show up on time to every meeting.
2. Expectations—Have and demonstrate clear expectations.
3. Education—Arrange training as necessary.
4. Encouragement—Take time to encourage employees at every opportunity.
5. Empowerment—Empower and enable your employees.
6. Extending trust—Trust your employees.

Food for Thought

1. Do you follow the three-step process to generate a cost reduction plan for new products?
2. Do you generate an annual GPM improvement plan describing cost reduction steps?
3. What three major steps are you going to take this year to improve organizational and employee productivity?

PART

C

INSTILL A PROBLEM-SOLVING CULTURE

CHAPTER 9

Follow the Implementation Model

One of the major challenges for management is to get things done. I have developed a model based on my over thirty-five years of experience to do just that. A culture that solves problems and achieves goals is necessary for world-class performance. You may recognize some of this material from other parts of the book. The repetition is intentional to emphasize the importance of getting things done effectively and efficiently.

How to Get Things Done

Implementation is the sum of
Discipline + Set of Behaviors + Systems and Techniques

Discipline is the gap between goals and accomplishments. How do you develop discipline in the organization? You instill an execution culture.

Set of Behaviors: To change the behaviors, establish
Continuous Improvement Culture + Culture of Recognition
and Appreciation

Systems and Techniques: These are the foundation to build a world-class-performing organization:

a) goals system
b) corporate problem-solving model
c) alignment of organizational elements

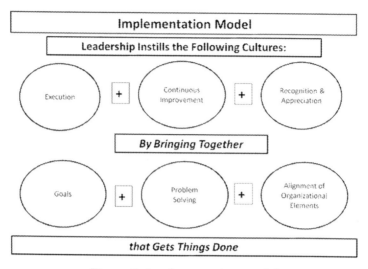

Figure 3: Implementation model.

Cultures

> *The only thing of importance that leadership*
> *does is to create and manage culture.*
> —Edgar Henry Schein, MIT

What does "culture" mean? Simply speaking, it means shared goals, values, beliefs, attitudes, and practices of an organization. As we can see from figure 3, the first step in getting things done is to instill appropriate cultures within the company's overall culture. Organizations will succeed only if they have instilled the right culture. This means the top leadership must make a commitment to make culture their top priority. *Culture impacts performance, and leaders impact culture.*

It is very difficult to change or instill culture. To change or instill the culture is like a turnaround situation, and turnarounds take time, persistence, and continual effort. There are three main reasons that make it difficult to change and instill culture.

Barriers to Instilling Any Culture

❖ There is a myth in almost all organizations that there is not enough bandwidth (resources) to make changes. This is like saying you don't have time to sharpen the saw to be able to continue cutting the wood efficiently.

❖ Some organizations do not know how to go about it. Methodology such as this can help.

❖ There is always resistance to change. This book shows three simple steps that you can take to overcome resistance to change.

How can top leadership instill the first row of the model in figure 3—the execution, continuous improvement, and recognition and appreciation cultures? The first step is to make the unwavering commitment to instill the culture. The second step is to make it a major corporate initiative. The way you do that is to set this initiative as one of the three wildly important goals (WIGs) for the year. WIGs are discussed in chapter 6 under Step 5A: Master Execution.

Cultural change efforts are typically most effective in situations of crisis or when the leader changes. Executives should spend the right amount of time to understand the organizational culture. The hardest area for any executive to understand is organizational culture. It is very difficult to act upon cultural issues and to get it right. Most executives struggle with implementing material changes to organizational culture because culture is hard to change and measure. The challenge posed by culture is that many executives do not have accurate ways to measure or even describe it. The following sections review the three cultures from the model in figure 3.

Execution Culture

Chapter 6 in step 5A: Master Execution described a ten-step process to instill the execution culture. The execution culture is very critical for organizational success. To emphasize this fact, the three most important steps are repeated here:

How to Instill the Execution Culture

- ❖ Put an operations infrastructure in place.
- ❖ Employ a unique management style.
- ❖ Establish a change management process.

1. *Put an operations infrastructure in place.*
   You need to put an operations infrastructure in place to get things done right consistently throughout the organization. You will follow this process for each major initiative the organization undertakes. The process works as follows:

   1) Come up with a strategy for a given initiative.
   2) Put processes/systems in place to support the strategy.
   3) Set and monitor goals. Set, monitor, and track appropriate KPIs.

   If the effort does not turn into results, something is wrong. If this is the case, look into the following:

   - the objectives, targets, and strategies that were set
   - the actions being pursued
   - the people involved

   Once you look into the above points, revisit the three steps of operations infrastructure and make necessary adjustments.

2. *Employ a unique management style.*
   The unique management style has three elements: setting goals, focus, and tracking and driving results.

Setting goals. We will talk more about how to go about setting and achieving goals later in this chapter. While establishing goals, focus on setting learning goals, not just output goals.

Focus means two things. First, it means

Follow
One
Course
Until
Successful.

Secondly, it means to apply the Pareto principle, a principle named after economist Vilfredo Pareto that specifies an unequal relationship between inputs and outputs. The principle states that, for many phenomena, 20 percent of invested input is responsible for 80 percent of the results obtained—that is, the lion's share of results come from a small amount of effort. Twenty percent of your time will produce 80 percent of useful results. Twenty percent of your decisions will lead to more than 80 percent of your success and happiness. Twenty percent of customers will bring in 80 percent of revenue.

The bottom line is to identify only a few activities that you should pursue because they will lead to greater results. Investigate the problem. Ask questions. Investigative thinking is 80/20 activity. We already discussed a detailed process to focus organization efforts in chapter 7 under step 5B of the methodology.

Tracking and driving results. Tracking is your mechanism for communicating clearly and unambiguously the performance that is occurring at the enterprise, business unit, department, and individual levels. Tracking increases accountability among your employees. If you have the right people on your team, peer pressure is a powerful accountability force.

To track means to measure where you are and where you want to go. Measure things that are most important to you. If you want to improve something, you have to measure it. Here you want to keep track of major KPIs to improve your performance. For example, KPIs such as product yields, inventory, customer returns, and outgoing quality. *Remember— when progress is measured, progress improves. When progress is measured and reported, improvement accelerates.*

Tracking increases accountability. Great people want to see progress. Limit metrics to three items and make tracking visible. Why do we want to track?

- to eliminate surprises to improve decision making
- to minimize subjectivity and emotion in addressing performance
- to provide a performance scorecard

To drive means to identify obstacles and problems that prevent you from achieving the desired performance and taking actions. Since 85 percent of the problems are system-, process-, or communications-related, you want to identify process or system problems and generate plans to fix them. Focus on fixing such problems rather than fixing people!

3. *Establish a change management process.*
   Change is the law of life. And those who look only to the
   past or present are certain to miss the future.
   —John F. Kennedy

Why do you want to establish a solid change management process in your organization?

Thirty years of research by leadership guru Dr. John Kotter have proven that 70 percent of all major change efforts in organizations fail.[9]

The change management process deals with how to handle change. For example, how to initiate and implement a major initiative. There are two change drivers: opportunity and pain. Most of the time, it is pain that drives the change. In most cases, change is met with resistance. The trick is to figure out how to overcome the resistance to change. If you pursue the following process, you will have a much higher probability to overcome the resistance to change and will be able to implement the change successfully.

Where does the resistance come from?

- lack of information
- fear
- people trying to control the situation

---

[9] Dr. John Kotter, *The 8-Step Process for Leading Change.* (Harvard Business School Press, Brighton, 1996).

Pursue the following process to increase the probability of overcoming the resistance:

The change management process.

❖ Keep employees informed of the change and avoid surprises completely. To get buy-in from unwilling employees, it will serve you well to begin by explaining to them the reasons behind the change. This step is important if you are to motivate any unwilling staff members. It is important that you communicate your change program (as much of it as is possible) on a regular and timely basis. No one likes to be surprised.

❖ Get employees involved in generating action items, making decisions, and implementing the change. Give them tools to manage the change and time to actually solve the problems. Involve a variety of employees in the planning, decision making, and monitoring stages of the change strategy. By including members across the organizational hierarchy, you are more likely to gain their support/buy-in and less likely to surprise anyone.

❖ Create champions at all levels who support the change wholeheartedly. Find individuals throughout the organization who can serve as champions of your change program. These individuals carry influence among other staff members; their ability to convince others of the merits of the desired change strategies will make them effective proponents of the program.

In order to increase your chances of overcoming resistance to change, you must do the following:

• Embed things into processes. That is, change management practices and techniques must be built in in everything you do.
• Realize the fact that a workforce that is flexible, open-minded, and interested in learning is far better than a workforce that is determined to keep doing it the old way.
• Encourage resistance to change. Why?
  • Resistance is a driving force. The act of resisting, in itself, is a tremendous source of energy.

- When people resist, it is your opportunity to show that you are hearing them.
- If you yourself are afraid of resistance triggers, you will meet even stronger resistance from your people. Instead, if you encourage resistance as a natural process to accompany change, compassionately showing that you hear people's fears, your stakeholders will be a lot more inclined to trust you rather than to oppose you.

Continuous Improvement Culture

What does "continuous improvement" mean, and how do you instill a continuous improvement culture? Continuous dissatisfaction must characterize the leader and the organization culture, which results in continuous improvement and upgrading.

Continuous Improvement Means the Following:

- ❖ continuously raising the bar to improve company performance
- ❖ continuous dissatisfaction on the part of the organization and its employees, so they will never be satisfied as far as making improvements
- ❖ constantly improving on existing metrics and KPI values

In order to instill a continuous improvement culture, the top management must create a continuous improvement environment by showing employees the benefits of improving performance and by explaining the importance of the change. This means that top leadership must continuously and consistently communicate with the employees by establishing effective communications channels.

How to Instill a Continuous Improvement Culture

- ❖ Handle the change management process described in methodology step 5A effectively.

❖ Introduce and implement a simple yet powerful six sigma-based problem-solving tool, the Paynter chart, discussed in detail on page 96.

❖ As discussed in step 5A, all supervisory employees should become proficient in employing the unique management style to make continuous improvements.

The key to embedding a capacity for continuous performance improvement in any organization is to hardwire it into the infrastructure. The methodology shows how to do this. Where will the journey of continuous improvement take you? The journey will take you to operational excellence, or the point at which each and every employee can see the flow of value to the customer and fix that flow before it breaks down. This definition of operations excellence applies to every level and every person in the organization.

Here is an example of how to go about instilling a continuous improvement culture.

Deryl Sturdevant, President & CEO, Toyota—Canada, stated:

> What happens in Toyota's culture is that as soon as you start making a lot of progress toward a goal, the goal is changed, and the carrot is moved. It's a deep part of the culture to create new challenges constantly and not to rest when you meet old ones. Only through honest self-reflection can senior executives learn to focus on the things that need improvement, learn how to close the gaps, and get where they need to be as leaders.[10]

---

[10] Deryl Sturdevant, "(Still) Learning from Toyota," *McKinsey Quarterly* (February 2014).

Pursue the following steps to put a continuous improvement infrastructure in place:

- Set up systems for sharing knowledge and best practices to ensure that improvements in one area are quickly adopted in relevant areas across the organization.
- Establish processes to identify and capture opportunities for improvement that enable employees at any level to change things for the better.
- Come up with methods to facilitate continuous learning that give the organization a chance to pause and take stock of what's working, what isn't, and what to do about it.
- Provide dedicated expertise to ensure continuous improvement activities get the attention they deserve.

Culture of Recognition and Appreciation
> *When we fail to appreciate, we begin to depreciate.*
> —Kent Krive

Top leadership must realize that talent management and retention is one of their biggest responsibilities and challenges. The ten-step operational efficiency improvement process described in part B will help instill a culture of recognition and appreciation. The top three important steps follow:

Important Steps to Instill a Culture of Recognition and Appreciation

- ❖ Recognize the fact that employees are the biggest asset an organization has.
- ❖ Find out what employees want and show them how to get it.
- ❖ Trust and value your employees. Make them feel genuinely important.

In short, create a recognition culture where everyone counts.

How do we know that the culture is being instilled and maintained?

First, you need to audit the culture to measure the progress and to maintain the culture. One of the ways to do this is to create metrics and track and drive. For example, one of the metrics could be getting things done versus doing things right.

Secondly, while developing the culture, make sure that you pursue the following elements of culture development:

Elements of Culture Development

- ❖ clear, objective standards of performance applied equally to all
- ❖ development opportunities for all employees
- ❖ constructive feedback to shape future performance

Organizations that do not reward smart experimentation and smart risk-taking, even when the outcome is unsatisfactory, may risk losing valuable, courageous, innovative, and creative people to other organizations.

Food for Thought

1. How would you describe your organization's culture? Are you happy with it?
2. What systems and/or processes are in place to instill and sustain your given culture?
3. How do you measure the impact of culture change?

The Foundation to Build a World-Class-Performing Organization

As noted near the beginning of this chapter, implementation is the sum of three elements: Discipline + Set of Behaviors + Systems and Techniques. By instilling the three cultures discussed above, organizations can take care of two (discipline and set of behaviors) of these three elements. The third element is taken care of by setting up the systems discussed below to build the foundation of a world-class-performing organization. The foundation is made up of the following key elements:

> ## Foundation of a High-Performing Operation
>
> ❖ goals system
> ❖ problem-solving system
> ❖ system to align organizational elements

Goals System: There are several books written on how to set and achieve goals. Evidence from numerous studies and experiments shows that setting explicit, challenging goals significantly enhances motivation and work-related performance. Goals must be tied to the vision and mission of the organization. Goals have more impact when combined with feedback, and even more so when combined with selected training to close performance gaps.

Here we are talking about putting in place a meaningful goals system that will start getting desired results by design and will be the backbone of a world-class-performing organization. It will allow you to execute major initiatives for your organization to make significant improvements in a given area.

Major Elements of Goals Systems

❖ Set three wildly important goals (WIGs) every year.
❖ Use the SMART goals model.
❖ Rigorously analyze goals and assumptions.

What is a WIG? Simply speaking, a WIG is a goal that can make all the difference in your organization. A WIG can also be called a BHAG (big hairy audacious goal), as defined by James Collins and Jerry Porras in their book *Built to Last: Successful Habits of Visionary Companies.*[11] This is the goal to kick off and implement a key corporate initiative that will have a major impact on improving execution, improving cost structure, or developing operations expertise. The most important task is to set wildly important goals (WIGs) and rigorously track the progress of these goals. We discussed WIGs extensively in part B.

The SMART goals model is a very powerful tool that is used to make meaningful progress. The model is used for ease of understanding, tracking, and execution. Extra time spent during the goal-setting process to use this model will provide significant returns.

I highly recommend that the organization use the SMART goals model while setting WIGs. Since WIGs are the major initiatives that the organization is undertaking, it is critical that the business spend a significant amount of time using the SMART model during the goal-setting process.

The SMART goals model defines what the goals should be:

SMART Goals Model

Specific & **S**tretched

Measurable & sometimes **M**emorable

Agreed upon & **A**mbitious but **A**chievable

Relevant & **R**ealistic & **R**obust

Time-Specific & **T**errific

Each element of the model is self-explanatory. In general, when you set goals, make sure that each goal meets the above requirements. At times, you can have qualitative goals that may not meet all the requirements.

---

[11] Jerry Porras and James Collins, *Built to Last: Successful Habits of Visionary Companies* (New York City: William Collins, 1994).

Problem-Solving System: This topic is discussed in detail in chapter 11 (step 9).

System to Align Organizational Elements: This topic is discussed in detail in chapter 3 (step 2).

Food for Thought

1. What process do you use to generate three major initiatives for the year?
2. Are your organization's supervisory employees trained in using the SMART goals model?
3. Do you have a well-defined goal-setting process for the entire organization?

CHAPTER 10

Expose Harsh Realities
(Breakthrough Thinking)

If you find a path with no obstacles, it
probably does not lead to anywhere.
—Frank Clark

The process to expose harsh realities will help you generate a meaningful plan. A plan is not a plan until it specifies how you will deal with setbacks, obstacles/potential problems, and backup plans (strategies). Remember— sometimes people have a tendency to paint over problems instead of solving them.

In regard to setting goals and objectives, what does "analyze goals and assumptions rigorously" mean? It means to systematically expose the reality of the situation to accomplish the goal. A goal must be backed up by a plan. By fully examining "why not" (for example, why won't you reach your goal?), you will identify barriers to your goal.

To uncover such issues, you need to follow a process to expose the reality. This is the most important step of the goals system. However, most executives do not go through this step during the goal-setting process. Executives do not realize its importance and hence do not take any time to go through this step. I have personally sat in several executive staff meetings and board meetings but have hardly ever seen this step followed thoroughly.

Benefits of the Process to Expose Harsh Realities

1. Improve the efficiency of business conversation.
2. Raise the level of critical thinking.
3. Get terrific results.
4. Increase accountability.
5. Own responsibility.
6. Come out as a united team.
7. Build collaboration.

How do you go about systematically exposing harsh realities?

If you want to disrupt the status quo, if you want to make progress and find new ways of thinking and doing, you need to ask questions. Questions are the first link in the chain of discovery and innovation. *Good questions inform; great questions transform.* Good leaders ask great questions that inspire others to dream more, think more, learn more, do more, and become more.

Demand conflict from team members and let them know that they are going to be held accountable for doing whatever the team ultimately decides. Demanding conflict means getting different opinions or points of view for a given topic. Peer-to-peer accountability is the primary and most effective source of accountability on a leadership team. Ensure that all members place a higher priority on the team they are a member of than the team they lead in their departments. That is, all members must put the organization's interests ahead of their own. Discuss failures openly and cordially in a meeting. This is the only way to create solutions. Taking actions involves taking risks and the courage to take on criticism.

In short, exposing harsh realities means having vigorous fact-based dialogues, a characteristic of high-performing teams.

A Process to Expose the Reality of the Situation While Setting Goals

- Ask: Is this a goal or a task?
- Does it meet SMART model requirements? (See model in step 7.)
- Meticulously discuss hows, whats, whens, and so on, including questioning each element of the SMART model and discussing/questioning assumptions.
- When questioning, find a solution and subject it to every kind of challenge it might conceivably encounter, and then correct any and all possible shortcomings.
- The answers to the questions above will result in excellent plans and/or powerful goals.
- The most important questions to ask are what else can we do and what can we do differently, what's next, and why not? These questions will inspire people to think more, learn more, do more, become more, and dream more.
- After questioning, redefine the goal (more likely than not, you will have to redefine the goal).
- Generate action items from the discussion or generate subgoals, if necessary.
- Gain commitment, and ensure accountability.
- Mercilessly follow through; track periodically and relentlessly provide constructive feedback.
- Develop a culture of "Always ask what's good for the organization" to avoid departmental politics.
- Handle these discussions professionally.

Asking questions is an important step. Questions ignite imaginations, avert catastrophes, and reveal unexpected paths to brighter destinations. The right questions do not allow people to remain passive.

Warren Berger, the author of *A More Beautiful Question*, praises inquiry's ability to trigger divergent thinking, in which the mind seeks multiple, sometimes nonobvious, paths to a solution. Asking good questions and doing so often "opens people to new ideas and possibilities," says Berger.[12]

The next time you have the opportunity to make a goals presentation, be prepared to answer the above questions, that is, have a game plan ready instead of pulling numbers and facts out of thin air.

Food for Thought

1. How much time do you spend exposing the reality of the situation during the goals review process? A minimal or a significant amount of time?
2. How do you go about uncovering issues during the goals setting and review process?
3. Is questioning a part of your organizational culture?

---

[12] Warren Berger. *A More Beautiful Question: The Power of Inquiry to Spark Breakthrough Ideas* (Bloomsbury, London, March 2014).

CHAPTER 11

Utilize a Problem-Solving Model

Individuals solve problems; geniuses prevent them.
—Albert Einstein

Problems are a normal part of any business. Solving problems leads to change, and change often leads to the result we are striving for.

You need to have a systematic approach to solve your organization's complex problems. One of the best things you can do is to follow the corporate problem-solving model described below. The model is based on my own professional experience, as well as my research on top problem solving methodologies.

Corporate Problem Solving Model

Problem solving requires new approaches. - Albert Einstein

1. Problem Solving Strategy: What to change, what to change to, how to make the change.
   Seeing the problem is harder than solving the problem.

2. Problem Solving Approach:
   A. Use a process to expose the reality of situation to make real progress.
   B. Utilize a 5 question structure to get to the bottom of the issue.
   C. Establish Corporate Continuous Improvement Process
   Judge a man by his questions rather than his answers. - Voltaire

3. Problem Solving Tool: Utilize Paynter Chart.

4. Progress Tracking: Come up with key leading and lagging performance indicators.

Figure 4: Corporate problem-solving model.

1. *Problem-Solving Strategy*

    One of the most difficult situations any organization faces is to determine what needs to be changed. This is so because it is harder to see the problem than to solve it. How can you see the problem? One of the best ways to do this is to analyze where you are, where you want to go, and how. This means to perform an organization performance risk assessment. The result of this assessment will tell you what major initiative the organization needs to undertake. The major initiative should tell you what to change, what to change to, and how to make the change. The initiative will become one of the WIGs for the year that you can track and drive.

2. *Problem-Solving Approach*

    There are three problem-solving approaches that can be used to solve complex business problems. The first approach of exposing the harsh reality of a situation focuses on asking great questions to uncover hidden issues and to make meaningful progress. This was discussed in the previous step and is repeated here. The second approach, called the "Five-Question Structure," focuses on getting to the bottom of issues to find real solutions. The third approach discusses how to instill a continuous improvement culture in your organization.

Use a process to expose the reality of the situation to make real progress.

This process is almost the same as the one that we discussed under the goals system.

A Process to Expose the Harsh Reality of the Situation

- Ask this question and write down the answer: What's the situation?
- What are the different elements of the situation?
- Meticulously discuss hows, whats, whens, and so on, including questioning each element and discussing/questioning assumptions.

- When questioning, find a solution and subject it to every kind of challenge it might conceivably encounter, and then correct any and all possible shortcomings.
- The most important questions to ask are what else can we do, what can we do differently, what's next, and why not? These questions will inspire people to think more, learn more, do more, become more, and dream more. After questioning, rewrite/describe the situation in detail, including assumptions.
- Generate action items from the revised situation. The result will be the major initiative the organization should undertake.
- Gain commitment, making sure to follow up on accountability.
- Persistently follow through; track periodically.

Utilize a five-question structure to get to the bottom of the issue.

While exposing the reality of the situation, you may want to ask the following questions:

1) What's the best thing that happened to our organization, or what's working for us?
2) What makes that the best thing or what makes that work?
3) What would be ideal for our organization? (Future vision.)
4) What's not quite right yet? (Get to the problem.)
5) How can we close the gap? (What resources or knowledge will we need?)

Establish a corporate continuous improvement process. There are five components of a corporate continuous improvement process. The goal of this process is to continuously improve after solutions to problems have been identified.

The Corporate Continuous Improvement (CI) Process

1) Corporate success axioms—the five Cs system
2) Performance improvement methodologies
3) Product improvement system
4) Employee development

5) Problem-solving (quality) tools and process improvement methodologies

   1) *Corporate success axioms—the five Cs system:* In order to kick off a corporate continuous improvement process, you need to put the five Cs system in place. It is the foundation of the corporate continuous improvement process. All employees should be trained on and have explained to them the importance of these five elements.

Commitment—Top leadership needs to make a commitment to this process.

Communicate the commitment to the troop.

Culture—Change/instill the desired culture.

Continuous improvement—Make this a corporate mantra.

Customer (internal/external) satisfaction—Make this everyone's top priority.

Top leadership needs to put appropriate systems and processes in place to make the five Cs system work. Some of the systems and processes we have already discussed, and others will become obvious throughout the book. Some people refer to the five Cs system as TQM (total quality management).

   2) *Performance improvement methodologies:* Performance improvement methodologies describe how to improve overall performance of the organization in everything the company does. The emphasis is on the process improvement. The major methodologies are as follows:

   ❖ Lean Process
   ❖ Six Sigma
   ❖ Strategic Continuous Improvement Process

There are many quality related books written on Lean and Six Sigma. Here we will focus on the key elements of the above three to put appropriate processes in place to kick off these methodologies.

Lean Process: A lean process is one that centers attention around reducing complexity. You do this by focusing on the following:

❖ Eliminate waste.
❖ Eliminate variation.
❖ Add value.

Eliminate waste means to improve yields (e.g., product yield, process yield), eliminate variation means to make use of SPC to bring processes under control, and add value means to focus on the separation of value-added and non-value-added work and eliminate non-value-added work and the costs associated with it.

Six Sigma: Six Sigma focuses on reducing process defects. A defect is anything that does not meet the customer expectation. Six Sigma uses statistics and is a data-driven approach to reducing defects. The Paynter Chart problem-solving tool that is discussed in detail on page 96 uses the Six Sigma approach. There are two main methodologies that are used: DMAIC to reduce defects from the existing process and DMADV to design a defect-free process.

DMAIC stands for Define, Measure, Analyze, Implement, and Content or Control. DMADV stands for Define, Measure, Analyze, Design, and Verify.

Strategic Continuous Improvement Process: We already discussed this process under the corporate problem-solving model. This process is based on the book *The Theory of Constraints* by Eliyahu Goldratt.[13] It is called "strategic," meaning this is the approach you should take to make any continuous improvement. It has three considerations:

❖ what to change

---

[13] Eliyahu Goldratt, *The Theory of Constraints* (Great Barrington: North River Press, 1999).

❖ what to change to
❖ how to cause the change

3) *Product improvement system:* This system shows how to produce quality products cost-effectively. The major elements of the system are as follows:

❖ right design first time process
❖ new product introduction (NPI) process
❖ product yield improvement system

Right Design First Time Process: This means, as quality guru Dr. Edward Demming said, that quality has to be built in or designed in, not inspected in. This is the first step where product cost reduction begins, as quality product will not need product redesigns; hence, it will save cost and will reduce time to market, which will increase profitability. This process is described in chapter 8 under step 6.

New Product Introduction (NPI) Process: This process will define who is going to do what and when. It will help shorten product development time and hence will reduce time to market. Also, it will help tremendously to produce quality product, as various groups responsible to design and manufacture the product will be constantly working together.

The key elements of the NPI process are as follows:

• procedure/guidelines to develop new products
• productization meeting to track and drive the progress of new product development
• product verification process
• product validation process
• product qualification process
• product testing process
• product yield analysis and enhancement process
• product documentation

Product Yield Improvement System: Improving product yields is a major challenge. The first major challenge is to design the product right the first time. The next major challenge is to improve product yields on time. The product yield improvement system is described in detail in chapter 8 under step 6.

4) *Employee development:* We talked about employee development under the "Culture of Recognition and Appreciation" in chapter 9, step 7.

3. *Problem-Solving Tool*

One of my bosses introduced me to this tool, called a Paynter chart. Paynter charts are probably one of the most unique and informative formats utilized in presenting information. They were first developed at Ford and have become common in businesses around the world. Their power lies in their ability to pull together key pieces of information to assist in understanding and solving a given problem. The Paynter chart is based on Six Sigma, as well as on the Pareto principle, which focuses on the areas of priority and quickly puts them in a simple graphical form by subgroups. It helps your team focus their efforts where they can have greatest impact. It allows you to determine the composition of each bar for troubleshooting or spotting trends.

I have used this tool successfully to improve productivity, on-time-delivery performance, product yields, customer returns, and so on. The way I use this tool is as follows:

Each manager or engineer generates this chart for anything he or she wants to improve, such as productivity, product yield, and so on. They bring this chart to a weekly meeting, which I chair. We discuss the issues and track progress of their action items in this meeting.

The tool, the Paynter chart, that we used looks like this:

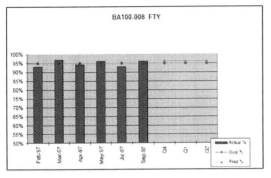

	Feb-97	Mar-97	Apr-97	May-97	Jul-97	Sep-97	Q4	Q1	Q2
Actual %	93%	97%	94%	96%	93%	96%	----	----	----
Goal %	95%	95%	95%	95%	95%	95%	95%	95%	95%
Pred %							96%	96%	96%

Problem	Vdd	Gain	Delta
Impact	1%	1%	1%
Cum	1%	2%	3%

Key Actions / Milestones			
Action / Milestone	Respons	Start	Complete
Improve final test yield on BA100-008	BKM	Jan-97	
1. Vdd: tighten limits at sort	BKM	Jan-97	Feb-97
take data on A510 look at distribution. adjust limits.	BKM	Aug-97	Oct-97
2. Gain: add tests at sort.	BKM	Jan-97	May-97
3. Delta gain: add tests at sort.	BKM	Jan-97	May-97
Note: FT Vdd limits tightened & Delta gain tests added due to MPC failures.			

Impact Progress (Sep)					
Apr	May	Jun	Jul	Aug	Sep
	1%				
	0%				
	0%				

As can be seen from the above diagram, the tool is divided into four quadrants. As you know, in order to improve anything, you have to measure it. The top left quadrant is called the "Measurement" quadrant. In this example, the product yield is measured monthly and plotted. The top right quadrant is called the "Pareto" quadrant, where you plot the top three to five major failure modes/defects/reasons that constitute the total failures/defects/reasons for the last month. The bottom left quadrant is called the "Action" quadrant. Here you show the action item for each of the major Pareto failures, the person responsible to take the action, and when the action will begin and end. The fourth quadrant is called the "Impact" quadrant, where you can track the impact of your action items as to whether you made the expected impact after completing the action item.

5) *Problem-solving (quality) tools*

- Paynter chart (developed by Ford and discussed in this book)
- control chart

- defect measurement
- Pareto diagram/Pareto analysis
- process mapping
- statistical process control (Cpk's)
- tree diagram
- fishbone diagram
- scatterplot (scattergraph)
- stratified sampling
- histograms
- check sheet

Process improvement methodologies

- Six Sigma
- Just In Time (JIT)/Kanban
- 5S
- cellular manufacturing
- total productive maintenance
- preproduction planning (3P)
- Lean Enterprise Supplier Networks

4. *Progress Tracking*
   In order to make improvements, you need to track progress. One of the best ways to track performance progress is to use leading and lagging performance indicators, as discussed in the methodology in step 5A.

Food for Thought

1. Are "Lean" and "Six Sigma" principles understood and used by your organization?
2. Is your company using a company-wide problem-solving tool to make continuous improvements in all areas of the business? Do you use a systematic approach to solve your organization's complex problems?
3. Do you have a well-documented and well-defined NPI process? How effective is it?

CHAPTER 12

Have a Management System in Place

Ineffective management allows the wrong things to happen. Give managers the tools they need to succeed.

A manager's ability to make the right things happen is not an inherent skill; no one is born a manager. Although management does require some talent, it also requires learning certain disciplines. These management disciplines extend a manager's ability, allowing the manager to accomplish more than would have been possible without these tools.

Management Disciplines

There are seven learned disciplines of management:

1. *Planning* is bringing the future into the present so that you can do something about it now. When you go through the process of goal setting, you are working on the planning process.
2. *Organizing* means to maximize resources and results by making sure that the required resources are available and by arranging activities in such a way that resources are used effectively and efficiently.
3. *Measuring Performance.* If you want to improve anything, you have to measure it. The measurement of the performance gives immediate feedback and forces you to take immediate actions. There are three ways to measure performance: (a) time-based, (b) outcome-based, and (c) relational-based.

4. *Executing* means taking concrete actions and making sure that activities are assigned to resources effectively. Execution is the key to getting things done.

5. *Following up* fosters accountability and produces desired results. It encourages employee cooperation. It is a vehicle to create actionable feedback.

6. *Real-Time Reporting.* The advantage of real-time reporting is that it identifies best practices, and best practices bring about best performance outcomes.

7. *Problem Solving.* Solving problems is what effective management does. To be effective, follow the problem-solving model discussed in this book.

In order to make things happen and to produce the desired results, I use a very effective three-step management style that encompasses the seven learned disciplines.

1. Set goals.
2. Focus.
3. Track and drive.

If you instill this style in your supervisory level staff—from your first line supervisor all the way up to top management—the overall effectiveness of your organization will increase manyfold. This style was described extensively in part B of the methodology under the "Employ a Unique Management Style" portion of step 5A in chapter 6. Management's ability to make use of this style company-wide will determine how successful the organization is.

Three-Step Management Style Description

1. *Set Goals:* We already talked about setting and achieving goals in chapter 9, step 7: Follow the Implementation Model.

Management disciplines learned through this step are as follows:

- *planning*
- *organizing*
- *measuring performance*

2. *Focus:* We also talked about this topic in chapter 9, step 7: Follow the Implementation Model.

Management disciplines learned through this step are as follows:

- *planning*
- *organizing*

3. *Track and Drive:* Again, we talked about this topic in chapter 9, step 7: Follow the Implementation Model.

Management disciplines learned through this step are as follows:

- *executing*
- *following up*
- *real-time reporting*
- *problem solving*

Food for Thought

1. Are you using *focus* to its maximum advantage?
2. What are your organization's strengths and weaknesses?
3. Have you put in place a well-defined management system for your organization?

CHAPTER 13

Methodology Execution Strategy

Leo Tolstoy, the Russian novelist, famously wrote, "Everyone thinks of changing the world, but no one thinks of changing himself."

Tolstoy's dictum is a useful starting point for any executive engaged in organizational change. Many research studies show that organizational change is inseparable from individual change. Simply put, change efforts often falter because individuals overlook the need to make fundamental changes in themselves. Building self-understanding and then translating it into an organizational context is easier said than done, and getting started is often the hardest part.

Methodology Execution Strategy

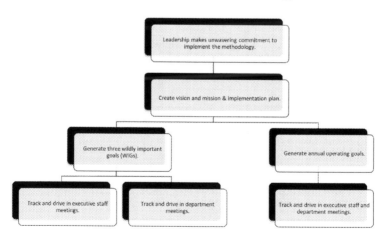

Many companies move quickly from setting their performance objectives to implementing a suite of change initiatives. Be it a new growth strategy or business-unit structure, or the rollout of a new operational-improvement effort, such organizations focus on altering systems and structures and on creating new policies and processes.

To achieve collective change over time, actions like these are necessary but seldom sufficient. A new strategy will fall short of its potential if it fails to address the underlying mind-sets and capabilities of the people who will execute it.

McKinsey[14] research and client experience suggest that half of all efforts to transform organizational performance fail either because senior managers don't act as role models for change or because people in the organization defend the status quo. In other words, despite the stated change goals, people on the ground tend to behave as they did before. Equally, the same McKinsey research indicates that if companies can identify and address pervasive mind-sets at the outset, they are four times more likely to succeed in organizational change efforts than are companies that overlook this stage.

In order to bring operational transformation, are you willing and ready to change yourself and to identify and address pervasive mind-sets of your people? If yes, the first step in executing the methodology is to come up with the game plan to do these two things and execute this plan.

The next step is to make unwavering relentless commitment as we discussed under part A of the methodology. It is repeated below to emphasize its importance.

What does "unwavering commitment" mean?

- ❖ To make operational improvement efforts a success, the top leadership needs to make fundamental changes in themselves. They need to change their own mind-sets and the mind-sets of their teams.
- ❖ Senior managers must act as role models.

---

[14] Nate Boaz and Erica Ariel Fox, "Change Leader, Change Thyself." *McKinsey Quarterly*, no. 4 (2014). Retrieved from McKinsey & Company.

❖ Since the employees in the organization defend the status quo, the leadership must follow a change management process. The organization must identify and address pervasive mind-sets at the outset to make the change effort a success. McKinsey research indicates that if you do this, you are four times more likely to succeed in organizational change efforts than are companies that overlook that stage.

❖ The CEO must dedicate at least 10 percent, on average, of company resources to the operational improvement initiative to build and sustain the long-term health of the organization.

❖ Devise a system to measure culture change and then track and drive.

❖ In order to gain commitment from all employees, come up with a performance-based rewards system.

❖ Make the tough decisions.

How do you know you have made unwavering commitment? If you have made a written plan of actions, including WIGs, and put in place measuring and monitoring mechanisms to monitor the progress, then you can say you are ready to bring about the operational transformation.

The third step is to review the progress periodically. Hold separate review meetings for short-term and long-term objectives in order to ensure that the company maintains a balance between operational improvement (for example, tactical strategies, productivity) and long-term health/growth (e.g., tactical strategies, and capability management).

To bring about change, the leader should ask this question: Are we introducing new policies, procedures, systems, and processes and/or using any models? The trick is to find simplicity within the complexity of accelerating the change.

Remember the following:

❖ Poor implementation is the enemy of change.

❖ Change is a process, not a singular thing.

Food for Thought

1. Does your business need operational transformation?
2. What new policies, procedures, systems, and processes have you put in place to achieve operational transformation?
3. Do you role-model desired changes?

CHAPTER 14

Methodology Case Study

The Challenge

Improve the gross profit margin (GPM) of high-tech products (analog and mixed-signal semiconductors) (220 products, eight product lines) to achieve competitive advantage.

What Did We Accomplish?

How Did We Use the Methodology?

(1) Methodology Part C
(2) Introduction Chapter
(3) Methodology Part B
(4) Methodology Part B
(5) Methodology Part B
(6) Methodology Part C

What Quantifiable Results Did We Produce?

Improved Gross Profit Margin (GPM) by 5%, saving millions of dollars over 2 years

This is proof that the ten-step methodology works and can really improve your organization. The improvement in our gross profit margin positioned the company to make other improvements over the next few years, improving the bottom line and the corporation's health, and the success of the changes we implemented inspired the staff to continue to find ways to improve.

Conclusion

We have covered a lot of ground in this book. We have explored the principles that are essential to achieving organizational excellence. The methodology steps are the principles of greatness that work wonders in normal times, as well as in the face of chaos, disruption, uncertainty, and colossal change.

The details of the methodology may seem common sense, but they are not always common business practice. As a business leader, ask yourself this: Have we integrated these solid management principles into company rules, processes, policies, and/or procedures? The book will inspire you to ask great questions to your staff. A good leader knows good questions inform while great questions transform!

As a leader, once you study, implement, and practice these principles, you will take your organization to greater heights. Remember—lack of management discipline correlates with decline, and passionate adherence to sound management discipline correlates with ascent.

This book outlines guidelines that, when followed, will produce desired results in the shortest possible time for years to come. It's easy to get so busy running your organization that you don't think about its future and how to continuously improve your organization's performance. The methodology was developed to provide a road map about making a plan to plan.

Thinking long term is not only hard because the future is ambiguous, but also because the here and now is so emphatic and conspicuous. In the present, everything must get done now. Even when immediate needs have been met, the future remains distant and fuzzy.

As the leader of your organization, you must make an unwavering commitment to bring operational transformation. Once you do this, you must take time away from short-term demands. This means to hide yourself for a few days to generate the plan to implement the methodology.

The methodology will be your road map that will help you consider what to plan for and when and how to plan for it. Rigorous thinking and disciplined behavior sustained over a long period of time will help make things happen.

Can you commit at least 10 percent of your organization's time every week to build a world-class-performing organization? If you can, you will see the results you desire.

Make building a world-class-performing organization the top corporate initiative by using appropriate communications channels and by integrating it into the company's policies and practices. You can use organizational performance risk assessment to identify the symptoms and root causes of underperformance and to generate a game plan for each root cause.

Convert your three major initiatives into three WIGs for the year and use the appropriate methodology to achieve them.

During the track and drive phase of the execution plan, make necessary adjustments based on the information at hand to make real progress. If necessary, get help from a business coach with operations expertise.

Finally, if you follow the above process and guidelines discussed in this book and execute the methodology, you will have created a culture of accountability, discipline, and systems. Your organization will be a well-oiled organization that endures. You will produce desired results day in and day out. You will do well by doing good. You will improve short-term performance as well as will build and sustain the health of the organization. Your organization will have the following benefits:

- ❖ The execution culture will be your competitive advantage.
- ❖ You will have achieved a world-class cost structure.
- ❖ You will have built your company's organizational health.

I hope this book has inspired you to use the methodology to achieve organizational excellence. Study the ten steps discussed in the book. Memorize them. Use them at every opportunity you get as a part of your daily routine at work.

Good luck!

GLOSSARY

- **accountability:** The obligation of an individual or organization to account for its activities, accept responsibility for them, and disclose the results in a transparent manner. Also, a series of steps that, when followed consistently, will produce consistent results every time. Accountability is one of the biggest challenges business leaders face, but it can also be one of the most important factors leading to success. Accountability starts with purpose.
- **best business practices:** Understanding your operations and cost thoroughly, getting the best return on investment, satisfying your customers, and understanding that you are never done with the job.
- **competitive advantage:** Uniqueness and value of your people, culture, processes, products, and services from your customer's perspective.
- **cost:** Total Cost = Fixed Cost + Variable Cost. Variable Cost → Direct and Indirect Costs.
- **discipline:** Training to act in accordance with rules. Discipline is the gap between goals and accomplishments. It is difficult to do.
- **enduring:** Standing the test of time.
- **ethical:** Doing the right thing.
- **ethics:** Ground rules or basic principles that a person will not breach.
- **excellence:** A journey toward perfection. The result of caring more than others think is wise, risking more than is safe, dreaming more than others think is practical, and expecting more than others think is possible.

- **excellent:** Having achieved exceptional performance.
- **methodology:** A set or system of methods, principles, and rules for regulating a given discipline.
- **metric:** Parameters or measures of quantitative assessment used for measurement, comparison, or to track performance or production.
- **moral:** Having a clear ethical compass.
- **performance:** The execution or accomplishment of work.
- **process:** Techniques to run a business that can be applied to any content (e.g., decision making or conflict resolution, the approaches to which are the same in both health care and cement businesses).
- **quality:** In manufacturing, a measure of excellence or a state of being free from defects, deficiencies, and significant variations.
- **strategy:** A plan, method, or series of maneuvers for obtaining a specific goal or result.
- **system:** A set of interacting or interdependent components forming an integrated whole. The key to driving a high-performance culture.
- **urgency:** For high-performing companies, urgency is the disciplined focus on a handful of compelling priorities that are executed with purpose, commitment, and immediacy.
- **value:** The degree of improvement to the client represented by the achievement of the objectives. These may be qualitative or quantitative.

Sources Used by the Author for General Guidance

1. Goldratt, Eliyahu. *The Goal*. Great Barrington, MA: North River Press, 1984.
2. Goldratt, Eliyahu. *The Theory of Constraints*. Great Barrington, MA: North River Press, 1999.
3. Covey, Stephen. *The 7 Habits of Highly Effective People*. New York City: Free Press, 1989.
4. Porras, Jerry, and James Collins. *Built to Last: Successful Habits of Visionary Companies*. New York City: WilliamCollins, 1994.
5. Peters, Thomas, and Robert Waterman. *In Search of Excellence: Lessons from America's Best-Run Companies*. New York: HarperCollins, 1982.
6. Hill, Napoleon. *Think and Grow Rich*. Cleveland: The Ralston Society, 1937.
7. Bossidy, Larry, and Ram Charan. *Execution: The Discipline of Getting Things Done*. New York City: Crown Business, 2002.
8. Connors, Roger, Tom Smith, and Craig Hickman. *The Oz Principle*. Upper Saddle River, NJ: Prentice Hall, 1994.
9. Kilts, James, Robert Lorber, and John Manfredi. *Doing What Matters: How to Get Results That Make a Difference*. New York City: Crown Business, 2007.

10. Turnock, Judith, and Michael Hyter. *The Power of Inclusion: Unlock the Potential and Productivity of Your Workforce.* Hoboken, NJ: Wiley, 2005.

11. Soundview Webinars on Books (summary.com):

1) *Self-Reliant Leadership*—Jan Rutherford.
2) *Creating Urgency and Growth in Nanosecond Culture*—Jason Jennings.
3) *The Pause Principle*—Kevin Cashman.
4) *Excellence in Motion*—Susan Guiher.
5) *Brief*—Joe McCormack.
6) *Change-Friendly Leadership*—Robert Dean Duncan and Stephen M. R. Covey.
7) *Beating the Global Odds*—Paul A. Laudicina.
8) *Extreme Productivity*—Robert Pozen.
9) *Predictable Success*—Les McKeown.
10) *Triggers: Creating Behavior That Lasts*—Marshall Goldsmith.
11) *Out Think*—G. Shawn Hunter and Tim Sanders.
12) *Stop Selling Vanilla Ice Cream*—Steve Van Remortel.
13) *Inspired People Produce Results*—Jeremy Kingsley.
14) *Little Bets*—Peter Sims.
15) *Leadership Sustainability*—Dave Ulrich and Norm Smallwood.
16) *The Trust Edge*—David Horsager.
17) *Leading So People Will Follow*—Erika Andersen.
18) *The 31 Practices*—Alan Williams and Alison Whybrow.
19) *The 80/20 Manager*—Richard Koch.
20) *Accountability*—Greg Bustin.
21) *Stacking the Deck*—David Pottruck.
22) *Blindsided*—Bruce Blythe.
23) *Serial Innovators*—Claudio Feser.
24) *Beyond Performance*—Scott Keller and Colin Price.
25) *Becoming Your Best*—Steve Shallenberger.
26) *Good Leaders Ask Great Questions*—John C. Maxwell.
27) *Pitch Perfect*—Bill McGowan.
28) *The Learned Discipline of Management*—Jim Burkett.

29) *Focus*—Daniel Goleman.

30) *Triple Crown Leadership*—Robert Vanourek and Greg Vanourek.

31) *The Purpose Economy*—Aaron Hurst.

32) *Low-Hanging Fruit*—Jeremy Eden and Terri Long.

33) *Finding the Next Steve Jobs*—Nolan Bushnell and Gene Stone.

34) *Picture Your Business Strategy*—Christine Chopyak.

35) *Follow the Leader*—Emmanuel Gobillot.

36) *Getting to It*—Jones Loflin and Todd Musig.

37) *The Cost of Emotion in the Workplace*—Vali Mitchell and Kristen Noakes-Fry.

38) *Smart Trust*—Stephen M. R. Covey and Greg Link.

39) *The Inclusion Breakthrough*—Fredrick Miller and Judith Katz.

40) *How to Be Exceptional*—John Zenger and Joseph Folkman.

41) *The Accidental Creative*—Todd Henry.

42) *The Laws of Subtraction*—Matthew May.

43) *The 4 Disciplines of Execution*—Chris McChesney and Sean Covey.

44) *All In*—Adrian Gostik and Chester Elton.

45) *The Strategist*—Cynthia Montgomery.

46) *The ACE Advantage*—William Schiemann and Peter Cappelli.

47) *Lead with a Story*—Paul Smith.

48) *Zero-Time Selling*—Andy Paul.

49) *Change Anything*—Kerry Patterson, Ron McMillan, and Al Switzler.

50) *Likonomics*—Rohit Bhargarva.

51) *Taking People with You*—David Novak.

52) *SNAP Selling*—Jill Konrath.

53) *The Advantage*—Patrick Lencioni.

54) *Breakthrough Branding*—Catherine Kaputa.

55) *The Synergist*—Les McKeown.

56) *Lead by Greatness*—David Lapin.

57) *Speaking as a Leader*—Judith Humphrey.

58) *The Reinventors*—Jason Jennings.

59) *The Power of LEO*—Sudhir Chowdhry.

Printed in the United States
By Bookmasters